Twayne's English Authors Series

Sylvia E. Bowman, *Editor*

INDIANA UNIVERSITY

Alfred Tennyson

TEAS 110

132

121

154

139— ~~[illegible]~~ Tenny's attempt a monologue

Alfred Tennyson

By JAMES D. KISSANE
Grinnell College

Twayne Publishers, Inc. :: New York

Library of Congress Catalog Card Number: 73-120018

MANUFACTURED IN THE UNITED STATES OF AMERICA

To Nancy

Preface

The plan of this book about Alfred Tennyson aims to meet the difficulties inherent in an attempt to survey comprehensively but in a limited space the work of a prolific and versatile poet. A chronological treatment, though the readiest, seemed also the most routine and unexciting prospect; to organize the book around some central thesis, on the other hand, would have made balance and the requisite breadth almost impossible to achieve. I have, therefore, chosen to consider Tennyson's poetry mainly by genres.

The first and last chapters present, respectively, a capsule history of Tennyson's reputation as a poet and my own conclusions. Well-informed students of Tennyson will find Chapter 1 traversing especially familiar ground, and they might do well to pass it over for the three middle chapters that constitute the bulk of the volume. These take up the broad categories into which Tennyson's verse seems obviously to fall: lyric, narrative, and dramatic (the latter including monologues and the monodrama along with the plays).

Though such grouping may be obvious, it is not exact. As one writer has observed, "Tennyson never wholly abandoned one genre when he moved on to another; he simply absorbed the old into the new. Consequently, almost all of his longer poems are hybrid in form and style. Tennyson appears to have approached composition in terms of local generative drives—lyric, dramatic, or narrative—instead of formal structures." [1] Accordingly, chapters 2, 3, and 4 are concerned not so much with neat and rigid groupings as with these "generative drives" and the particular poems they engendered. Convenience rather than taxonomical precision was, in any case, my purpose; a consideration of Tennyson's poetry by types throws certain important topics into sharper relief and even approximates, in a rough way, the course of his poetic development. Yet I am conscious of there being many more potentialities for fruitful speculation and investigation in a generic approach to Tennyson's poems than I have been able to explore. In fact, the way nineteenth-century poets in general responded to all traditional formal classifications—not only the larger categories but the lesser ones—is a subject I do not think has had sufficient study.

As I give a last anxious thought to what I have written before committing it to such fate as its readers assign, it strikes me that my estimate of Tennyson's poetry may on balance seem less favorable than it actually is. Somehow one feels obliged to make a clean breast of one's reservations, whereas admiration is a thing to be more discreet about; also it simply is less difficult to find words of blame than praise. These are the perversities of the critical effort. The fact is, however, that writing this book has increased my respect for and enjoyment of Tennyson's poetry by a considerable measure. And that fact has added both pleasure to the task and regret for my deficiencies in fulfilling it.

JAMES D. KISSANE

Grinnell College

Acknowledgments

I should like to acknowledge the kindness of the following for permission to quote:

City Lights Books, San Francisco, for the lines from Allen Ginsberg's "Howl."

Houghton Mifflin Company, Boston, for use of the Cambridge Edition of Tennyson's poetical works.

Indiana University Press for passages from *The Devil and the Lady and Unpublished Early Poems,* edited by Sir Charles Tennyson.

Wesleyan University Press for the quotation from Donald Davie's "Remembering the Thirties."

Thanks are also due to my colleagues in the English Department at Grinnell College for their encouragement and advice, especially Mrs. Carol Parssinen, who made many helpful suggestions for trimming the manuscript to the required length. Finally, I am grateful to my English 332 classes in 1966 and 1968 for their patience and interest.

Contents

Chronology

1809 Alfred Tennyson born August 6 at Somersby, Lincolnshire, the fourth of twelve children (eight sons, four daughters) to the Reverend George Clayton Tennyson and Elizabeth Fytche Tennyson.

1820 Alfred and his brother Charles leave Louth grammar school. From that time, until he enters Cambridge, Alfred is educated by his father.

1827 *Poems by Two Brothers* published anonymously. Charles and Frederick Tennyson contribute poems to the volume as well as Alfred. Dr. Tennyson, Alfred's father, sent to France on account of his failing health. Alfred enters Trinity College, Cambridge, with his brother Charles.

1829 Becomes a member of the "Apostles" ("The Cambridge Conversazione Society").

1830 *Poems, Chiefly Lyrical* published. Goes to Spain with Arthur Hallam to bring financial aid to the rebels opposing Ferdinand VII.

1831 His father dies; Alfred leaves Cambridge without taking a degree. Arthur Hallam's review of *Poems, Chiefly Lyrical* appears in the *Englishman's Magazine.*

1832 *Poems* published (dated 1833). Tours the Rhineland with Hallam. One of Alfred's brothers, Edward, suffers a mental collapse; another, Charles, becomes addicted to opium.

1833 John Wilson Croker assails Tennyson's *Poems* in the *Quarterly Review*. Arthur Hallam dies at Vienna, September 15; Tennyson receives the news October 1.

1833–1837 Lives with the family at Somersby. Series of more or less serious attachments to Sophie Rawnsley, Rosa Baring, and Emily Sellwood.

1837–1842 Tennyson family removes to High Beech in Epping Forest, later to Tunbridge Wells, then to Boxley. Alfred's engagement to Emily Sellwood is broken by her family. His patrimony is lost through the failure of a woodworking scheme in which Tennyson had invested it. Makes the acquaintance of a number of literary and otherwise notable personages, including William E. Gladstone, Samuel Rogers, Thomas Carlyle, John Forster, Walter Savage Landor, William C. Macready, and Aubrey deVere.

1842 *Poems* (2 vols.) published.

1843 Enters a hydropathic hospital for a serious nervous depression.

1845 At the instigation of Henry Hallam, Arthur's father, Tennyson is granted a government pension of two hundred pounds by Sir Robert Peel.

1847 *The Princess* published.

1850 *In Memoriam* published anonymously. Marries Emily Sellwood. Named Poet Laureate by Queen Victoria, as the successor of William Wordsworth.

1852 Hallam Tennyson born.

1853 Rents Farringford (which he buys in 1856) on the Isle of Wight.

1854 Lionel Tennyson born. "The Charge of the Light Brigade" is published and cheers the troops before Sebastopol.

1855 *Maud, and Other Poems* published.

1859 *Idylls of the King* ("Enid," "Vivien," "Elaine," "Guinevere") published.

1862 Publishes a new edition of the *Idylls of the King* with a dedicatory poem to the late Prince Consort; invited to Osborne to meet Queen Victoria.

1864 *Enoch Arden, Etc.* published.

1867 Purchases the site for Aldworth, his summer home in Sussex.

1869 The Metaphysical Society, with Tennyson one of the charter members, organizes and begins holding meetings. Aldworth completed. *The Holy Grail and Other Poems* published.

1872 *Gareth and Lynette Etc.* published.

1874 Turns to the writing of drama with *Queen Mary*.

1875 *Queen Mary. A Drama* published (produced the following year at the Lyceum Theatre).

1876 *Harold. A Drama* published (volume dated 1877).

1879 *The Falcon,* a one-act play, produced at St. James' Theatre.
1880 *Ballads and Other Poems* published.
1881 *The Cup* produced at the Lyceum Theatre.
1882 *The Promise of May* produced at the Globe Theatre.
1883 At Gladstone's urging, and in accordance with the Queen's wishes, accepts the peerage, becoming the first Baron Tennyson.
1884 Gilbert and Sullivan's opera *Princess Ida,* a "respectful parody" of *The Princess,* is produced at the Savoy. *Becket* published. (The play had been printed in a shorter version in 1879; it was produced by Irving in 1893.)
1885 *Tiresias and Other Poems* published.
1886 Death of Tennyson's son Lionel while returning from India. *Locksley Hall Sixty Years After Etc.* published.
1889 *Demeter and Other Poems* published.
1892 *The Foresters* produced in New York and published. (The play had been written in 1881 as a result of a visit to Sherwood Forest.)
1892 Tennyson dies October 6. Buried in Westminster Abbey October 12. *The Death of Oenone, Akbar's Dream, and Other Poems* published posthumously.

CHAPTER 1

The Reputation

> People are almost always silent when one quotes good Tennyson. They prefer it to be awful, and then they can shout "My God!"
>
> G. B. Stern

DO YOU know," Gerard Manley Hopkins wrote to a college friend in 1864, "a horrible thing has happened to me. I have begun to *doubt* Tennyson." [1] Hopkins, who in so many ways was to be Tennyson's antitype among Victorian poets, was only twenty at the time; and everyone knows how irreverent undergraduates can be—even those who become Jesuit priests. Nevertheless, this mock confession is noteworthy, for in it are epitomized the inevitable contraries with which any consideration of Alfred Tennyson's reputation as a poet has to deal. Implicit is the acclaim, the adulation, that placed Tennyson, during his lifetime, among the greatest of England's poets; for Hopkins's pretended horror testifies to the very fame he disparages. But, on the other hand, just because the horror *is* bogus, it suggests the characteristic tone of Tennyson's detractors with their intimations that his eminence was not only unmerited but even slightly ludicrous.

The cult of Tennyson and the cult of Tennyson reaction, both adumbrated in Hopkins's letter, cannot but enhance the difficulty of a just appreciation of the poetry itself. Why not, then, ignore the history of the poet's reputation, with its alternations between the extremes of adulation and contempt, and approach his poems innocent of either bias? For one thing, there is a sense in which Tennyson's refulgence and eclipse constitute a legitimate part of his meaning and importance to English poetry. For another, it can hardly be supposed that many serious readers of Tennyson's poetry have, regarding the prejudices clinging to it, the kind of absolute innocence or open-mindedness that might be worth protecting. It is better, therefore, to give modest and preliminary attention to the matter of Tennyson's reputation, attempting to view it from a reasonable perspective, than to leave it as an unacknowledged yet somehow persistent element in one's consideration of the poetry.

I *"An Ardour of Gratitude"*

The earliest reaction to Tennyson's poetry that anyone knows about comes from a not unbiased source: his father. "If Alfred die," the Reverend George Tennyson said, in reference to poems his son had written before he was fifteen, "one of our greatest poets will have gone." [2] Even when Tennyson had become almost a living legend, he was never free from the stings of critical abuse; but the fact is that the kind of extravagant praise reported of his father—not by nature an effusive man—was never far from Tennyson's ear throughout his lifetime. The Tennyson family and their set at Somersby, Arthur Hallam and the other "Apostles" at Cambridge, and later his wife, along with friends and the constant admiring visitors to Farringford and Aldworth, kept steadily before the poet a sense of his genius and the duty he owed to it.

Moreover, Tennyson's reviewers, especially at the crucial points of his early career, were in numerous instances particular friends and champions of his work. Hallam, John Sterling, Richard Milnes, and James Spedding all helped to smooth the young poet's way with laudatory notices of his work. Possibly such encouragement so near at hand was unfortunate in making Tennyson a rather erratic judge of the value of criticism. He was not unduly swayed by flattery and remained suspicious of fame; but he often reacted strongly to quite irrelevant criticism, whereas some he might have pondered to good purpose—such as the discerning reservations of his friend Edward FitzGerald—he dismissed in bewilderment as the product of personal crotchet.

Tennyson was coauthor of one volume of poems (*Poems by Two Brothers* [1827]) before he went up to Cambridge; and he brought out another (*Poems, Chiefly Lyrical* [1830]) while he was there. These youthful productions, along with the award of the Chancellor's Medal for his blank-verse poem "Timbuctoo," made Tennyson something of a celebrity among young university intellectuals. Fanny Kemble, the sister of one of the Apostles—that group whose stimulation and influence was the most notable feature of Tennyson's residence at Cambridge—thought of him as "our hero, the great hero of our day." [3] And Tennyson looked the part, with his loose, powerful physique; dark gypsy-like face; and careless attire. Keats, Shelley, and Byron and all their promise were gone; Tennyson, to those who knew him, seemed their natural successor. But not until the volume *Poems*—dated 1833 though issued in December of the previous year—did Tennyson receive anything like wide attention; and the result came close to being disastrous. Critical opinion was not all unfriendly, but John Wilson Croker's notorious attack, published in the influential *Quarterly* and laced with derisive sarcasm, undoubtedly impeded Tennyson's rise to popularity and damaged his self-confidence.

Harold Nicolson exaggerates the influence of this review upon both Tennyson and the public in advancing his theory that the reception given the 1833 volume made Tennyson into a different kind of poet, one studious of avoiding critical displeasure and anxious to base his poetry upon "common interests" and "universal humanity." [4] It is at least true that Tennyson's next volumes, those of 1842, must stand as a remarkable literary comeback. In the interval, the so-called "ten years' silence," Tennyson had carefully revised his poems and added new ones; he was nursing his wounds, no doubt, but also perfecting his art. Meanwhile, references in the reviews and his own contributions to "keepsake" volumes indicate that Tennyson had not fallen into complete obscurity. Tradition has left us a picture of Tennyson during these years as struck dumb by cruel critics and by his sorrow for his dead friend Hallam; in any event, he did well to bide his time. Edward FitzGerald wrote in the spring of 1842 that Alfred was preparing to "publish such a volume as has not been published since the time of Keats: and which, once published, will never be suffered to die." [5] He was right. England had long been ready to acclaim a new voice in poetry, and the *Poems* of 1842 seemed to provide ample proof that this voice was Tennyson's.

The year 1842, marks, therefore, the beginning of Tennyson's success. Later critics who have decried his career as Poet Laureate have felt that, in a stricter sense, it was also the end. Such cynicism is extravagant, but the 1842 volumes did assemble a great many of Tennyson's best and most characteristic poems: "Mariana," "The Lady of Shalott," "Oenone," and "The Lotos-Eaters"—all published previously—and "Morte d'Arthur," "Ulysses," and

"Break, break, break"—among those published for the first time. Tennyson was informed that he had achieved a publishing sensation; Thomas Carlyle was rhapsodic in his praise; from America, Emerson, Hawthorne, and especially Poe voiced enthusiasm. As far as Tennyson's career itself is concerned, probably the most significant result of all this acclaim was that it began to compose itself into one clear call for him to apply his genius—now adequately demonstrated in a variety of briefer exercises—to the sustained effort, the monumental masterpiece. The poet's friend James Spedding, writing in the *Edinburgh Review*, expressed, almost sternly, the hope that Tennyson would "find a subject large enough to take the entire impress of his mind." [6] It must be supposed that such a vision of his poetic duty had its effect in drawing Tennyson into those subsequent attempts at substantial works in extended forms that leave even some of the poet's keenest admirers wild with all regret: *The Princess*, the *Idylls of the King*, and the chronicle plays.

The triumph of the *Poems* of 1842 was followed, strangely perhaps, by a lapse into such depths of hypochondria that Tennyson's life was all but despaired of. The cause was not entirely the strain of poetic endeavor and its attendant anxieties; Tennyson had invested his modest patrimony in a scheme for the manufacture of machine-carved furniture, and the project failed. His engagement to Emily Sellwood had been broken off; and financial ruin, added to the disapproval of the Sellwood family, left little hope of its being resumed. In 1847 *The Princess* appeared—that poetic freak, unlikely in subject as in narrative conception. Tennyson wrote grimly to FitzGerald: "My book is out and I hate it, and so no doubt will you." FitzGerald, always a staunch voice of loyal opposition amid the poet's less critical or more diplomatic friends, was as unimpressed as Tennyson feared: he judged *The Princess* "a wretched waste of power." "I almost feel hopeless about Alfred now," he sadly wrote.[7] FitzGerald's disappointment was shared by many, including Elizabeth Barrett Browning, who complained that the poem was unrhythmical and anti-feminist.[8] In its odd way, however, *The Princess* is thoroughly Tennysonian, a work typical of his genius in its defects and in its virtues; but it did little to advance his reputation.

The decisive year was 1850. Tennyson published *In Memoriam*, his most impressive work; he married Emily Sellwood on an advance against the proceeds from his long elegy; and he was appointed Poet Laureate of England. *In Memoriam* secured Tennyson's reputation; its early success (sixty thousand copies of the poem were sold in the first few months) was only the prelude to its eventual elevation to almost Scriptural status. Probably no other poem in English has made so prodigious an impression on contemporary readers. They saw in the poet's private anguish the reflection of their own troubling doubts. We are often reminded how the Victorians at mid-century confronted the belief-shattering discoveries of natural science with confusion and dismay. In Tennyson, however, they found their uncertainties nobly uttered and resolutely faced. In common with much of the greatest religious poetry, *In Memoriam* bears witness to the power of negative thinking; but it also expresses what Professor Sidgwick described as "the indestructible and inalienable minimum of faith." [9] This sense of the poem's having caught the residual essence of spiritual conviction in an age of scientific skepticism accounts largely for its overwhelming appeal to its Victorian audience.

Tennyson's marriage brought him domestic tranquility and, Mrs. Tennyson being the person she was, insured his productive application to his calling. It is tempting to see in her a chief cause of the increasing staidness of Tennyson's later career, though no doubt there was in him from the beginning a tendency to write in that elevated but uninspired style that Gerard Manley Hopkins termed "parnassian." All in all, it would not be unfair to conclude that Emily Tennyson abetted the duller rather than quickened the keener side of her husband's artistic nature.

Tennyson's appointment to the laureateship, the third memorable event of 1850, in a sense involves the other two: Prince Albert's admiration for *In Memoriam* is said to have persuaded the Queen to bestow the laurel upon its author, and any influence his marriage might eventually have had was surely in the direction of making Tennyson a more suitable Victorian laureate. Seldom has the title meant much, though the honor had gained something by Wordsworth's having borne it. In Tennyson's case, however, the laureateship was not simply a distinction of sorts; it became for once a precisely accurate designation.

In fiction, marriage and position are commonly the end of the story; and the same is approximately true of Tennyson's life. The years at Farringford and Aldworth were not uneventful; they brought forth the fruits of the Laureate's labors and the accumulation of honors, as well as the inevitable mortal sorrows and innumerable visits; but they produced nothing drastic or essential in the way of change. In considering Tennyson's reputation, we note a significant difference between the interest he had inspired up to 1850 and the fame he enjoyed and fretted over during the rest of his long life.

Tennyson's early poetry appealed mainly to the young intelligentsia, to those in the vanguard of taste. A whole generation came out of the universities quoting this poetry as a mark of sophistication. Later Tennyson had a much broader, more homely appeal. *In Memoriam,* with its acknowledgment of hard truths, on the one hand, and simple pieties, on the other, looks in both directions. *Maud* harks back in spirit to earlier work, whereas the best poems of Tennyson's old age are not really in the "Laureate" vein either. The poems that particularly gave his later reputation its dominant character are, of course, the *Idylls of the King* and *Enoch Arden.* The first was almost twenty-five years in attaining its final form and seemed to establish its author as the epic poet of his age; the second, Tennyson wrote in a fortnight, and it proved to many that their Laureate was indeed a Poet of the People. Medieval romance and domestic sentiment thus made up between them what most Victorians gladly enough took for God's plenty.

History and reminiscence have given us almost too many emblems of Tennyson's preeminence as bard and sage through the second half of the century—most of them tainted by sentimentality and a few tinged with irony. We have, for instance, the picture of George Eliot weeping as she and George Henry Lewes listened to the Laureate read them his verses about the guilty Guinevere; we are told of General Gordon in besieged Khartoum finding the reading of Tennyson a "great relief," though no help from Her Majesty's government reached him in time. And, of course, there were Tennyson's audiences and correspondence with the Queen—two lonely souls, each from a lofty eminence, exchanging with due formality moral platitudes and talk of the weather, comforting each other on their respective family sorrows. They were strangely kindred despite the incongruity that Max Beerbohm's caricature so wittily captures: the gaunt, gangling bard, high-domed and bearded; the stolid, Germanic figure of the Queen, with a face bland as a darning egg.

The picturesque solemnity of Tennyson's death and the dignity of his funeral and interment in Westminster Abbey were followed by a heightened reverence for the poet who even in life had become a legend. After his death, a flood of books sought to assess his place in English letters and insure its permanence. There is no easier way to suggest what Tennyson meant to his contemporaries than to list the titles of a few of these: *Tennyson: Poet, Philosopher, Idealist* (1893), *The Teaching of Tennyson* (1895), *Tennyson as a Religious Teacher* (1900), *Alfred Tennyson: A Saintly Life* (1900), *The Mind of Tennyson: His Thoughts on God, Freedom, and Immortality* (1903), *Glimpses of Tennyson and Some of His Relations and Friends* (1903), *A Child's Recollections of Tennyson* (1906), *The Social Ideals of Alfred Tennyson* (1906), *The Idylls and the Ages* (1907).

These tributes proclaimed not only the wisdom in his art but the goodness of his life. It was a goodness, moreover, rewarded by tangible recognition and material success. *The Tennyson Remembrance Book: A Memorial for the Poet's Reader Friends* (1893) begins in this vein: "To be always 'well to do' in the world, to live in that world for eighty-three years, to be esteemed in his day the chief of living poets, to be crowned the laureate of his land, to be buried in Westminster Abbey—this surely would seem to be the sum of all that is ideal in the career of a man of letters. And that in brief outline is the life-story of Alfred Tennyson, Poet Laureate of England."

Not all the praise was this fatuous; yet admiration for Tennyson at having so impressively "cashed in" was a recurring note, and along with it went the gratitude for Tennyson's respectability. The 1880s and 1890s brought disturbing currents from artistic quarters upon the English scene: the rank poisons of Zolaist Naturalism, Swinburne's blatant paganism, Pater's "art for art's sake," and other notions yet more French and more decadent, leading finally to the outrageous posings of Oscar Wilde. England was soothed by the example of Tennyson, illustrating that even at so late a date a poet may prove his genius as a Virgil rather than as a Villon.

But there was gratitude of a finer sort, gratitude not merely for the probity of the man but for his work in which, as Jowett said, his contemporaries "found expression for their noblest thoughts."[10] It would be perverse to discount or to belittle the importance attached to Tennyson's gift for explaining the age to itself. And what it saw revealed was not mere flattery either, as James Martineau's words imply: "In laying bare, as [Tennyson's poetry] does, the history of his own spirit, its conflicts and aspirations, its alternate eclipse of doubt and glow of faith, it has reported more than a personal experience: he has told the story of an age which he has thus brought into Self-knowledge."[11] And, a few days after Tennyson's death, the *Spectator* assessed his influence: "Those who were growing up, but were not yet grown up, in 1842, can hardly know how much of their ideal of life they owe to Tennyson. . . . They only know that they owe him very much of the imaginative scenery of their own minds."[12]

These words catch at something beyond Tennyson as teacher or even Tennyson as representative sensibility: he did more than interpret and verify the experience of his age—he transfigured it. From him came the images, the moods, and the characters that constitute the "imaginative scenery" with which for half a century Englishmen lived. His was the voice that created for his time a "way to feel" about life. A letter from William Makepeace Thackeray, praising the *Idylls of the King*, testifies as well as anything can to the effect of this power of emotional evocation upon the Victorians. The two bottles of claret that Thackeray admits having just drunk may account for some of his enthusiasm, but his tribute to the way "My Dear Old Alfred" had filled his friend's mind with images of the ideal is nonetheless instructive (*in vino veritas*): "Gold and purple and diamonds, I say, gentlemen and glory and love and honour, and if you haven't given me all these why should I be in such an ardour of gratitude?"[13]

II *Anti-Victorianism—and After*

If this ardor of Thackeray's seems peculiarly dated, the vehemence of the reaction against Tennyson is hardly less so. That is mainly because the critical disfavor his poetry suffered is so thoroughly bound up with the anti-Victorianism that was fashionable during the early decades of the twentieth century. As Paul Elmer More said, "Tennyson is the Victorian age."[14] No one disagreed. The old poet's admirers had insisted that the fact went far to explain his greatness; his detractors held it to be the most telling mark against him. However, this irony is only in part the result of differing estimates of the Victorian Age; it also involves a corresponding difference in what is meant by saying that Tennyson reflected his time. To some, as we have seen, he gave voice to its essential spirit, truly but inadvertently, by speaking from the depths of his own being. To others, he lulled the age by extolling more or less deliberately its own deadly virtues.

Though elaborated by the disillusioned post-Victorians, the case against Tennyson was by no means originated by them. The acclaim the Laureate won in his later career was far from universal. The 1870s especially produced a decline in his popularity. Browning's less familiar idiom was finally beginning its vogue; and the Rossettis, William Morris, and Swinburne stirred competing interests in the younger generation of poets. Then Tennyson turned to writing verse plays, an unfortunate diversion of his energies from areas to which his talents were better suited. Their appearances on the stage were taken as solemn cultural events, but few could deceive themselves into supposing they were in the presence of vital art.

Among his more discerning readers, moreover, considerable dissatisfaction with Tennyson's *magnum opus,* the *Idylls of the King,* began to develop as the separate idylls accumulated without seeming to promise a whole greater than its parts. Most of the slighting comments reflect a sense that the relation between ancient chivalry and Tennyson's manner of treating it was somehow false. Gerard Manley Hopkins called the *Idylls* "Charades from the Middle Ages"; George Meredith complained that King Arthur spoke like a curate and, anticipating much modern Tennyson criticism, blamed the public for having "corrupted this fine (natural) singer." Swinburne's attack, with its famous reference to "the Morte d'Albert, or Idylls of the Prince Consort," turned the tables on the Philistines by adopting a high moral tone against the Victorian Laureate. The love of Lancelot and Guinevere, Swinburne charged, has in Tennyson's poem the character not of a fabulous romance but of a sordid scandal: "Treated as he has treated it, the story is rather a case for the divorce-court than for poetry." [15]

Henry James provides the classic instance of disillusionment with Tennyson—one far from representative of the late 1870s when the two men were introduced, to be sure, but, as James himself might have said, portentous. Though Tennyson was, so James confesses, "the poet I had earliest known and best loved," his personal encounter with the shaggy, reticent old man constituted for the American novelist "the full, the monstrous demonstration that Tennyson was not Tennysonian." "Why in the name of poetic justice," James asks, "had one anciently heaved and flushed with one's own recital of the splendid stuff if one was now only to sigh in secret, 'Oh dear, oh dear'?"[16] Subsequently, proof that one was "on to" Tennyson came to be *de rigeur* for the true modern. A choice anthology of memorable remarks damaging to Tennyson could be compiled from the works of—to name but a few—Thomas Hardy, Samuel Butler, W. B. Yeats, James Joyce, and William Faulkner.

The dominant objection to Tennyson in the decades immediately following his death was that he indulged in obtrusive and earnest moralizing. This criticism was in line with the tenets of Estheticism and Symbolism which stressed the sensuous immediacy of "pure" poetry and the primacy of Beauty over Truth. After World War I, the emphasis changed: it was not that Tennyson's moral note had been excessive so much as that it was false. To the generation that bore the brunt of that hideous experience, the ideals on which they had been nurtured seemed at best a mockery and at worst a betrayal. Tennyson was, of course, a prime target of the general debunking of eminent Victorians that ensued.

The postwar prejudices are fairly reflected in two influential studies of Tennyson that appeared in 1923. One, *Tennyson: A Modern Portrait* by Hugh I'Anson Fausset, was avowedly iconoclastic; the other, Harold Nicolson's *Tennyson: Aspects of his Life, Character and Poetry*, a mixture of deft caricature and perceptive appreciation, must be classified as a salvage operation. In order to make any kind of case at all for Tennyson to his own generation, Nicolson felt obliged to vie with the Laureate's more determined detractors in depreciating much of the poetry the Victorians had admired; and the *Idylls of the King* Nicolson ignored altogether. Tennyson the conscious spokesman of a discredited era was alien, but Nicolson saw another aspect of the poet—more authentic, more congenial, perhaps more relevant—for which enthusiasm (especially when expressed with rhetorical finesse) was possible: "There are sudden panting moments when the frightened soul of the man cries out to one like some wild animal caught in the fens at night-time—moments when he lies moaning in the half-light in an agony of fear. And at such moments the mystical genius of Tennyson comes upon one in a flash. . . ." [17]

Along these lines Nicolson formulated the essential problem for Tennyson criticism: "If one could separate the two Tennysons—the prosperous Isle-of-Wight Victorian from the black, unhappy mystic of the Lincolnshire wolds—one would find in the former the secret of his weakness, and in the latter the secret of his preponderating and triumphant strength." [18] This formulation has had an immense influence in shaping subsequent estimates of Tennyson. If recent critical opinion has been steadily more favorable, that trend has been sustained mainly through the strategy of the "two Tennysons" theory—a strategy that allows the critic to undertake the rescue of Tennyson's reputation without having to slay the Hydra of anti-Tennysonian prejudice. What Nicolson referred to as a "duality of purpose and inspiration" has thus undergone a variety of mutations: Tennyson's "alien vision" has been examined, his "two voices" have been contrasted, his "two voyages" have been charted; he has been characterized as a "divided sensibility," and the "true dialectic" in his work has been described as "a tension between the insight of the solitary and the sense of the common and the social." [19]

As the "two Tennysons" theory has made a renewed interest in his work increasingly possible, certain ancillary claims regarding his poetry have become familiar. One of these, long acknowledged but given new authority, is the claim of Tennyson's technical virtuosity. We have T. S. Eliot's word for it that his versification is masterly and his ear the finest since John Milton. W. H. Auden, who has labeled Tennyson "undoubtedly the stupidest" English poet, goes even farther than Eliot in saying that, whatever his intellectual limitations, he had perhaps the finest ear of all.

A second point currently made in Tennyson's favor is that his best poetry is distinguished by an essential modernity. One critic has asserted that Tennyson's cultivation of the epyllion, or "little epic," "places him in close rapport with the art form of Joyce's *Dubliners*, Eliot's *Waste Land*, and Pound's *Cantos*" and that fortunately "our mid-century ways of thought and feeling" can discover in Tennyson a practitioner of "the sophisticated art of impressionism." [20] One of the finest essays on Tennyson produced by recent criticism, "Tennyson as a Modern Poet," insists "he is our true precursor." [21] Another study of Tennyson reiterates this note at its beginning: "We see in Tennyson almost the same dilemma that faces contemporary artists. Often when we read his poems we feel that Tennyson is of our age." [22]

For our fathers Tennyson was too Victorian for words; now we may apparently claim him as one of ourselves. Those who admire his poetry must be glad to encounter this opinion, yet where is the value in its being true for Tennyson in any sense that is not equally true of Shakespeare or Milton? Perhaps it would seem less important to insist upon Tennyson's modernity if the permanence of his achievement could be more confidently assumed.

However, this emphasis on modernity, whatever its relevance to the absolute worth of the poetry itself, has without doubt given vitality to recent Tennyson criticism. Finally, a further development of what Harold Nicolson diagnosed as the "reaction in favor of Tennyson" can be observed: the current inclination, in the name of a "balanced view," to restore for us the Tennyson that his contemporaries knew. On the one hand, Tennyson's virtually unqualified right to consideration as a *great* poet, a *major* poet, has been earnestly argued;[23] on the other, there is some recent tendency to treat sympathetically that more "public" side of Tennyson's poetry long considered, by most, a liability. Two titles, *Tennyson Laureate* and *The Pre-Eminent Victorian,* suggest the nature of this trend.[24]

It has even been reasonably proposed in one study that rather than Nicolson's two Tennysons—the mystical romantic and the staid Victorian—there are in fact three, and that it is the third who is the most genuine poet of all: "Tennyson's unconditional poetic success came only in those many poems (I think particularly of the lovely and too much ignored verses of occasion, of celebration, greeting, and elegy) where, as in *In Memoriam,* he speaks not as dark romantic or ancient sage but with the perfect clarity, tact, and grace of the great classical poet that in the truest part of him he was." [25]

"Action and reaction," as Tennyson himself dourly characterized the course of literary opinion—and his reputation has experienced such extremes of both as few English authors have known. At present, however, Tennyson's poetry enjoys solid but hardly overwhelming esteem. For some time it has ceased to be a mark of critical acumen to sneer at Tennyson, but it is not quite clear that having become a name for menthol cigarettes constitutes a vogue. Over the last several decades discussions of his poetry have repeatedly hailed Tennyson's rehabilitation, but that the point appears to require such reiteration is itself a cause for doubt. There is something in Tennyson's poetry that has withstood the most aggressive criticism; there is also something to that criticism which even the best of his poetry cannot fully disarm.

CHAPTER 2

The Lyric Poet

I *The Rhythmical Cry*

THE present chapter concerns itself mainly with poems belonging to a particular though certainly broad and heterogeneous category. It is well to remember, however, that the lyrical aspect of Tennyson's work is not confined to individual and autonomous poems that must be classed as "lyrics." There are also the songs that grace his longer poems and in some cases far outshine these larger wholes of which they are part: the blank verse lyrics in "Audley Court" and in *The Princess,* the intercalary rhymes added to the latter work, the song of the brook woven into the narrative of that name, a few songs scattered through the *Idylls of the King* and through the plays, and the arias of which the "monodrama" *Maud* largely consists. Moreover, lyricism is a quality that frequently distinguishes Tennyson's verse even when that verse is itself the vehicle of a basically narrative or dramatic conception. His preoccupation with the sounds and rhythms—the music—of language and his often uncanny skill in their manipulation are sufficiently evident throughout his poetry to promote the commonly taken view that Tennyson's gifts were essentially—almost exclusively—lyrical.

Elizabethan songs, the traditional ballad, and the poems of his Romantic predecessors taught Tennyson many an important lesson, but his most characteristic lyrics are marked by a Tennysonian something that really has no precedent in English verse. The quality is easier to apprehend than to characterize, for the variousness of Tennyson's art is not to be slighted. His individuality is, one must say, not so much a matter of style as of virtuosity. He effected no radical change in idiom, but he did bring the possibilities of versification to a new pitch of refinement. Style has to do with the quality that informs whatever gestures the poet makes, whatever effects he attempts. Virtuosity is a mastery of the means by which these various effects are achieved. Style incarnates temperament; virtuosity integrates technique. What one points to as characteristically Tennysonian, therefore, tends to be the uncommon concentration and artistry with which he uses common devices. The result is a poetry of studied ingenuity rather than exuberant invention.

No brief account of the technical side of Tennyson's lyricism can suggest his versatility or adequately represent his habits and skills in every aspect of versification, but a few generalizations and illustrations should be ventured. A concentration upon sound effects is surely among Tennyson's most striking qualities. Rhyme, being the most formalized of such effects, is no doubt the most obvious. The practice of many modern poets—Yeats most particularly—has developed in modern readers an admiration for subtlety and unobtrusiveness in the management of rhyme; Tennyson, on the contrary, treats rhyme not as a feature to be submerged but as one to be accentuated. In his rhymed poetry the lines are seldom run-on, and the end stop calls attention to the rhyme. Even more characteristic is his frequent rhyming of three or more consecutive lines, as in the triplet stanzas of "The Two Voices" and in the *a a a a b c c c b* stanza pattern of "Sir Launcelot and Queen Guinevere" and "The Lady of Shalott." In "The Ballad of Oriana" Tennyson links five lines with a single rhyme sound, injecting a one-word refrain after the first, second, fourth, and fifth rhymed lines.

The risks inherent in this almost fascinated exploitation of rhyme Tennyson could not always avoid. The song can lapse into the sing-song of doggerel:

> Who can say
> Why To-day
> To-morrow will be yesterday?

"O Darling Room," to cite that egregious example, is composed of three single-rhyme stanzas of six lines each. Such instances, however, suggest that infelicitous versification can seldom be divorced from the banality of the thought or the foolishness of the subject. On the other hand, it is an authentic mark of his skill that rarely in Tennyson's poetry does a rhyme seem to force an inept choice of word or the employment of unnatural word order.

Tennyson lavished equal attention upon other effects of sound. These tend toward the onomatopoeic. We hear in his poetry a rich diversity of natural sounds: the crash of surf, the moaning of doves and the murmur of bees, the soughing of the wind, a brook babbling over pebbles, birds crying from the high Hall-garden. Alliteration, a favorite effect, typically appears not randomly but in patterns of combinations, as in the 1–2–2–1 (*sl w w sl; c m m c*) configuration in the following lines:

A *sl*uice *w*ith blackened *w*aters *sl*ept
The *c*lustered *m*arish *m*osses *c*rept.

Or we have the 1–1–2–2–1–1/3–4–3–4 of

And "Ah," *s*he *s*aid, "to be *a*ll *a*lone,
To *l*ive *f*orgotten and *l*ove *f*orlorn."

In such lines Tennyson's sensitivity to the value of vowel sound variation is also apparent.

However, most sound effects—rhyme, assonance, alliteration—are forms of repetition; and repetition of all kinds so dominates Tennyson's verse as to be its virtual hallmark. Simple verbal repetition can make musical a single line: "Then let come what come may"; or an entire stanza may derive its intricate melody from repeated words, phrases, and lines:

Sweet and low, sweet and low,
Wind of the western sea,
Low, low, breathe and blow,
Wind of the western sea!
Over the rolling waters go,
Come from the dying moon, and blow,
Blow him again to me;
While my little one, while my pretty one sleeps.

If repetition thus brings music to Tennyson's poems, it can also serve as an element of form. We see this aspect in the way the words "Camelot" and "Shalott" rhyme in identical positions in each stanza (with one exception) of "The Lady of Shalott"—the two names representing the fundamental antithesis that is the theme of the poem. Even with so conventionalized a form as the sonnet (at which he did not excel) Tennyson employs in one instance a refrain-like repetition. That sonnet, "The Bridesmaid," introduces a slightly varied "refrain" at each formal break (lines 4, 8, and 14); and it plays upon the ambiguity of the motto, "A happy bridesmaid makes a happy bride," as the means of developing its subject.

It is, in fact, in Tennyson's use of refrains that his fondness for repetition finds widest scope. His lyrical refrains vary from the extremely simple to the remarkably ingenious, but nearly always they serve the ends of both euphony and form. The principle that seems most often to guide Tennyson in devising refrains is the interplay between similarity and diversity. Frequently, the refrain alters from stanza to stanza or, more dramatically, only in one or two significant instances. Within the refrain itself, Tennyson likes to employ every possible kind of repetition:

> Heavily hangs the broad sunflower
>   Over its grave i' the earth so chilly;
> Heavily hangs the hollyhock,
>   Heavily hangs the tiger lily.

An examination of the three forms of the refrain in the famous "Bugle Song" from *The Princess* reveals the intricacy with which Tennyson could combine reiteration and variation:

> Blow, bugle, blow, set the wild echoes flying,
> Blow, bugle; answer, echoes, dying, dying, dying.
> . . . .
> Blow, let us hear the purple glens replying,
> Blow, bugle; answer, echoes, dying, dying, dying.
> . . . .
> Blow, bugle, blow, set the wild echoes flying,
> And answer, echoes, answer, dying, dying, dying.

As Tennyson's way with refrains indicates, his fondness for repetition is one side of the coin of which resourcefulness and versatility are the other side. These last two qualities, by their nature, do not lend themselves to brief illustration; but they can at least be suggested by the kinds of ingenuity Tennyson exhibits, for example, in stanza forms. To consider the variations, both in rhyme and meter, that he practiced upon the four-line stanza is to gain some sense of his virtuosity. The famous and distinctive *In Memoriam* stanza (tetrameter, rhymed *a b b a*) comes first to mind, but there are many others. We find poems written in the standard tetrameter quatrain rhymed *a b a b* ("To J.S."); there is the modified ballad stanza, (*a b a b,* alternating tetrameter-trimeter; "The Goose," "The Talking Oak"); "The Palace of Art" is written in an alternate rhymed stanza whose lines are pentameter, tetrameter, pentameter, trimeter; in the stanza of "A Dream of Fair Women" the alternately rhyming lines are of five, five, five, and three accents, respectively. The elaborateness with which Tennyson designs longer stanzas is equally characteristic. A striking example is the song "A spirit haunts the year's last hours," whose two eight-line stanzas rhyme *a a b c c b b a* with a regular variation in line length between four, two, and one accents. To these stanzas is added a refrain (quoted above) of considerable complexity in its own right.

Line length is worthy of some notice in Tennyson's practice of versification. Two features can be cited as characteristic. One is Tennyson's tendency toward elaborate variation of line lengths within a single poem, either (as in the song just noted) with the regularity of a stanzaic pattern or with great flexibility (as in the "song" section of "The Hesperides"). These changes in line length produce much variation in the "velocity" of Tennyson's verse and often give to his rhythms a kind of syncopation. A second common feature of his verse in this respect is the frequent recourse to unusual line length. In some poems—the narrative "Merlin and the Gleam" and the lyric from *Maud* "Go not happy day"—the lines are remarkably short; but more commonly the lines are very long—longer, that is, than the "standard" English pentameter. "Rizpah," the "Northern Farmer" poems, "The Higher Pantheism," "The Voyage of Maeldune," and the opening section of *Maud* are all important poems written in verses of six accents; "Vastness" and the two "Locksley Hall" poems are in octameter.

Coleridge, when he had read one of Tennyson's early volumes, declared that "he has begun to write verses without very well understanding what metre is." [1] This remark has puzzled and amused admirers of Tennyson's skill as a versifier, especially in light of Coleridge's own unorthodox theories and practices. And yet it is probably true, judging by the kind of rhythms Tennyson produced, that he did not understand meter in quite the way his predecessors understood it. So far are many of his lyrics from following any common meter that the basic rhythmic unit seems to be not the metrical foot but the entire line. Despite the emphasis of rhyme that has already been mentioned and the frequent use of lines of only three accents or less, Tennyson usually succeeds in avoiding monotony and jingling by varying his lines with added unstressed syllables. And whereas unstressed syllables give his verse one kind of freedom—a loosening of the line and a rhythmic lilt—the piling up of stresses produces another: the freedom of sudden emphasis, the gathering of sudden strength—

/ / /
My very heart faints and my whole soul grieves
/ / //
At the moist rich smell of the rotting leaves

. . . .

/ /
Bury the Great Duke

. . . .

/ / / /
To waste his whole heart in one kiss

. . . .

/ / /
And one clear call for me

. . . .

/ / // / /
On the bald street breaks the blank day.

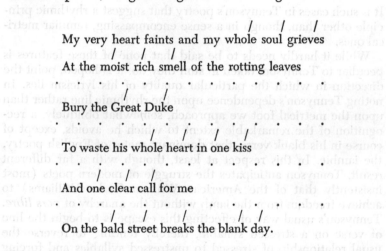

There are other ways Tennyson was able to achieve richer rhythms by freeing himself from metrical regularity. And yet meter is not cast aside or completely overridden. The song "Go not happy day" (from *Maud*), for example, is trochaic trimeter of the catalectic sort (the last foot is incomplete):

/ x / x / (x)
Pass the happy news,
/ x / x / (x)
Blush it thro' the West.

But this meter is challenged by a rhythm that works against it in a kind of counterpoint. This rhythm asserts a loose but decidedly two-stress pattern in opposition to the three-beat meter:

/ /
Rosy is the West,
/ /
Rosy is the South,
/ /
Roses are her cheeks,
/ /
And a rose her mouth.

It is such cases in Tennyson's poetry that suggest a rhythmic principle other than, though in a sense encompassing, familiar metrical ones.

While it hardly needs to be said that none of these features is peculiar to Tennyson, taken in sum they do, it is hoped, point the direction in which the particular quality of his lyricism lies. In noting Tennyson's dependence upon the rhythmic line rather than upon the metrical foot we approach, somewhat obliquely, a recognition of the remarkable extent to which he avoids, except of course in his blank verse, that dominant meter of English poetry, the iambic. In this respect at least, though with a far different result, Tennyson anticipates the struggle of modern poets (most insistently that of the American William Carlos Williams) to achieve freedom from the iamb without the anarchy of *vers libre*. Tennyson's usual way of effecting this escape is to begin the line of verse on a stressed syllable, thereby tending to reverse the usual relationship of stressed to unstressed syllables and forcing the line into a trochaic or dactylic rhythm, often a combination of the two:

/ x x / x / x
Gathering woodland lilies

. . . .

/ x x / x / x
Myriads grow together. . . .

The result is a characteristic dying fall so in accord with his customary lyrical moods:

/ x x / x / x / (x)
Heavily hangs the broad sunflower
/ x x / x x / x / x
Over its grave i' the earth so chilly

. . . .
/ / x / x / x /x /x /x
Blow, bugles; answer, echoes, dying, dying, dying.

In "The Captain" Tennyson creates a novel ballad rhythm by casting what is essentially a traditional ballad stanza into trochaic rather than into the usual iambic meter:

Then they looked on him they hated,
Had what they desired;
Mute with folded arms they waited—
Not a gun was fired.

One natural concomitant of this trochaic-dactylic emphasis is the frequency of feminine rhymes in Tennyson:

Willows whiten, aspens quiver,
Little breezes dusk and shiver.

But perhaps its most pervasive result is that these meters, being themselves a departure from the norm, promote irregularity and variety of the kinds we have already noted.

One final example may substantiate Tennyson's rhythmic virtuosity better than these generalizations about its many aspects. A stanza of the early poem "The Merman" runs as follows:

I would be a merman bold,
I would sit and sing the whole of the day;
I would fill the sea-halls with a voice of power;
But at night I would roam abroad and play
With the mermaids in and out of the rocks,
Dressing their hair with the white seaflower;
And holding them back by their flowing locks
I would kiss them often under the sea,
And kiss them again till they kiss'd me
Laughingly, laughingly;
And then we would wander away, away,
To the pale-green sea-groves straight and high,
Chasing each other merrily.

Twelve of these lines have four accents, but only lines two and five have an identical rhythm. There are, then, eleven different rhythmic variations within the four-stress pattern. Coleridge might well be excused for finding only metrical chaos in such variety, and it is true that one direction in which Tennyson's art matured was toward moderation in his attempts at rhythmic effect. But the point should be all the clearer that Tennyson, as a lyricist, was from first to last an artist fascinated with the materials of his art and greatly given to exercising his ingenuity upon them.

II *The Poet's Mind*

Alfred Tennyson probably never thought of himself as anything but a poet. At eight, he was covering his slate with blank verse in the style of James Thomson; by the age of eleven, he had written "hundreds and hundreds" of lines in imitation of Pope. Somewhat later he came under the spell of Walter Scott, composed a six-thousand-line epic in the meters of *Marmion*, and shouted passages of it into the night as he rambled the fields near Somersby. Nothing of this epic survives, but the blank verse drama he wrote at fourteen called *The Devil and the Lady* proves that his precocity could produce impressive results. Tennyson's earliest letters leave no doubt that he was almost painfully literary; but the most revealing indication of his youthful ambition and self-regard are the headings in one of his notebooks: "Vol. I 1820 *The Poetry of Tennyson;* Vol. II *The Lyrical Poetry of Tennyson* and; Vol. III *The Prose Writings of Tennyson.*"[2] "Well, Arthur," he confided to a younger brother, "I mean to be famous."[3] Without question, this fame was to be won by a faithful devotion to the muse.

That he was a poet, Tennyson always knew. But what, then, was a poet? Many of Tennyson's poems, especially among his early lyrics, have to do directly or indirectly with that question; but his certainty of vocation is hardly matched by an equal one as to the nature of the calling. Two poems from the 1830 volume are of obvious importance in this regard. One, "The Poet," advances the familiar Shelleyan claim for the poet as the trumpeter of prophecy, the unacknowledged legislator of the world.[4] He is a figure particularly fashioned for his large destiny: "Dower'd with the hate of hate, the scorn of scorn,/The love of love."

Blessed with special powers, the poet penetrates the mystery of life and death, the enigma of good and evil, and becomes a kind of interpreter of Divine Purpose: "The marvel of the everlasting will,/An open scroll,/Before him lay." The poet's thoughts are borne on wings of song until they fall "like the arrow-seeds of the field flower" to burgeon anew in a spring of Hope and Youth: "Thus truth was multiplied on truth, the world/Like one great garden show'd." Accompanying this burgeoning of poetic truths is a "rare sunrise" in which Freedom awakens and tyrannous rites and forms melt like snow. Next, Freedom speaks forth in thunder and lightning, "riving the spirit of man." Her power is not, however, a sword of wrath, "But one poor poet's scroll, and with *his* word/She shook the world."

The (probably coincidental) similarity of this earth-shaking influence to the vatic role proclaimed in Shelley's "Ode to the West Wind" and the *Defence of Poetry* makes it worth noting how little of Shelley's obsession with martyrdom is found in Tennyson's poem. The emphasis is on the poet's triumphant, if somewhat obscure, power rather than upon his adversity and immolation. It is the work of a fledgling artist who has felt no more of the frustrations of such a life than he has savored of its accomplishments, but who at any rate envisions his yet unachieved art in terms of a broadly social purpose.

"The Poet's Mind," another poem published in 1830, breathes a wholly different spirit:

> Vex not thou the poet's mind
>   With thy shallow wit;
> Vex not thou the poet's mind,
>   For thou canst not fathom it.
> Clear and bright it should be ever,
>   Flowing like a crystal river,
> Bright as light, and clear as wind.

The first strophe of "The Poet's Mind" reveals the same veneration for poetic powers manifest in "The Poet," but the concern is not for their universal dominion but for their exclusive preservation. Those divine gifts that were to shake the world in the other poem must be protected from the world in this one. The clear brilliance of the poet's thought is likened to fire in the first poem, illuminating, enkindling, or purifying whatever it touches; in the second poem, it is a crystal river, holy and mysterious, that must be guarded from contamination. If "The Poet" suggests Shelley, "The Poet's Mind" is reminiscent of Coleridge. Tennyson's incantatory

> Dark-brow'd sophist, come not anear;
> All the place is holy ground;
> Hollow smile and frozen sneer
> Come not here

recalls the aloof unapproachable sorcerer of "Kubla Khan" ("Beware! Beware! . . . Weave a circle round him thrice"); and of course the garden, the river, and the fountain have their counterparts in Kubla's domain.

But whereas the fountain in Coleridge's poem seems to be associated with demonic, or at least chthonian powers, Tennyson's explicitly has its ultimate source in "heaven above." This sacred fount, symbol of the poet's inspiration, leaps forth "with a low melodious thunder" that is, we are told, the "song of undying love." But such love is curiously incommunicable. In "The Poet," the "love of love" takes root in the common soil of humanity and transforms the world; in "The Poet's Mind" not only does the fountain's song of love fall on deaf ears, but there is no desire for it to do otherwise:

> And yet tho' its voice be so clear and full,
> You never would hear it, your ears are so dull;
> So keep where you are; you are foul with sin;
> It would shrink to the earth if you came in.

To be sure, this indictment is ostensibly aimed at some "dark-brow'd sophist" and not at everyman. Even so, the tone of spiritual and mental fastidiousness clashes with the humanitarian zeal of the other poem. A garden, that image with which Tennyson repeatedly associates the world of art, flourishes in both poems. In "The Poet" the seeds of truth sown by the poet make the world into "one great garden"—paradise regained. In "The Poet's Mind" the garden is very much the artist's private and jealously guarded preserve.

The power of poetry took, for Tennyson, at times the aspect of prophecy, at times, the form of conjuration. The poet was the prophet but he was also the magician. So even in his old age Tennyson could write of "The Ancient Sage" and also of "Merlin and the Gleam." By that time, however, the distinction had blurred: Merlin had become wise and bearded and had grown fond of oracular pronouncement. But in the younger poet these opposing conceptions form a crucial tension. Tennyson acknowledges the prophetic impulse in such early poems as "Perdidi Diem" and "Timbuctoo." In the former work the poet speaks to an unidentified auditor of his divine gift:

> You tell me that to me a Power is given,
> An effluence of serenest fire from Heaven,
> Pure, vapourless, and white,
> As God himself in kind, a spirit-guiding light,
> Fed from each self-originating spring
> Of most inviolate Godhead.[5]

This "godhead" may refer to nothing more special than the soul all men possess, but the language here—"fire from heaven," "spirit-guiding light," "spring"—identifies the soul's powers with those traditionally claimed for the vatic poet.

"Timbuctoo," which won for Tennyson the Cambridge prize medal in 1829, belongs to the category of dream-vision poetry and must be read as representing a poet's initiation into the mysteries of his hieratic art. Standing atop Gibraltar, the poet-figure muses on such fabled places as Atlantis and Eldorado; and he wonders if Africa, the modern *terra incognita,* might contain in reality a fair city, "Or is the rumour of thy Timbuctoo/A dream as frail as those of ancient time?" These meditations are disturbed by the visitation of "a young Seraph" who tells the poet that his sense is clogged with dull mortality and bids him "Open thine eyes and see!" The poet is transfigured: "I felt my soul grow mighty . . . I seem'd to stand/Upon the outward verge and bound alone/Of full beatitude." A dazzling city reveals itself to his rapt vision before he swoons in ecstasy.

Then the seraph speaks again: "There is no mightier Spirit than I to sway/The heart of man: and teach him to attain/By shadowing forth the Unattainable." He is a spirit that awakens in all men some glimmerings of the Ideal; the poet, however, has been particularly chosen: "I have given thee/To understand my presence, and to feel/My fulness; I have fill'd thy lips with power." Identifying himself as the Spirit of Fable, the seraph informs the initiate that the city he has just beheld must yield its glories to "keen Discovery"; this "mystery of loveliness" will be transformed into the mud huts of dreary actuality. The implication is, however, that the poet is to perpetuate the vivifying ideal.

But this view of the poet as an inspired voice of a higher truth is always liable, in Tennyson's poetry, to a change of focus that stresses not his value to humanity but his alienation from it. "The Mystic" (1830) treats of the visionary's divine insight in terms of the separation and "otherness" that it causes:

> Angels have talked with him, and showed him thrones:
> Ye knew him not; he was not one of ye;
> . . . .
> How could ye know him? Ye were yet within
> The narrower circle: he had wellnigh reached
> The last.

Moreover, the legendary city itself may represent less a vision to share with the world than a retreat from it. Thus in a poem from his Cambridge period Tennyson apostrophizes Troy, that city built to music, as a symbol of the imaginary kingdom of his art: "Ilion, Ilion, dreamy Ilion, pillared Ilion, holy Ilion/City of Ilion, when wilt thou be melody born?" (*UEP*). Tennyson's Ilion is his version of the pleasure dome; but, significantly, it is a "heavy walled, many towered" citadel, fortified against the world.

Sometimes the qualities of benefactor and alien appear together in Tennyson's depiction of the poet. "The Poet's Song" shows all creation entranced in admiration as he "sings of what the world will be/When the years have died away"—all creation but Man; for he has no place in this almost Blakean tableau. The poet passes by the town and seeks out a "lonely place" as his proper scene.

It must be assumed—evidence both within and apart from the poetry is commonly cited—that this conflict of attitudes regarding the nature and role of the poet reached its climax during Tennyson's years at Cambridge and as a result of his association with those earnest young men known as the Apostles. His sense of the poet's public obligation and opportunity was prodded by his friend Richard Trench's admonition that "we cannot live in art" and by Hallam's reminder that "poems are good things but flesh and blood is better." But it would be unfair to suppose that Tennyson's response was spiritless acquiescence. There was that in him which valued the poet's right to go his own way, his right—if it came to that—*not* to be earnest.

It is possible to see in "The Grasshopper" (1830) the emblem of the poet as a carefree singer of carols. Rejecting the insect's traditional connection with the Tithonus myth, Tennyson ascribes to him "No withered immortality/But a short youth sunny and free." He is the "Voice of the summer wind," free from sorrow or tears, to whom evil is irrelevant. But Tennyson is especially admiring of the grasshopper's invulnerability—he is a "mailéd warrior" with "shielded sides. . . . Armed cap-a-pie"—which leaves him free of fear and naturally makes him the envy of this shy and thin-skinned poet.

"An Idle Rhyme" (*UEP*) throws a more direct challenge in the face of moral responsibility:

> Oh, what care I how many a fluke
> Sticks in the liver of the time?
> I cannot prate against the Duke,
> I love to have an idle rhyme.

This poetic attitude seems to have begotten, at his best, the attractively languid escapism of "Recollections of the Arabian Nights" or, at his worst, the flighty affectations of the all too numerous "lady" poems ("Lilian," "Madaline," "Adeline," "Margaret," "Rosalind," and "Eleanore" are the most characteristic examples). "An Idle Rhyme" goes on to declare the muse owes her allegiance not to the concerns of the moment but to the ages. Shading into an almost solemn mysticism, the poem ends on a note that might have come from *In Memoriam:* "I cool my face in flowers, and hear/The deep pulsations of the world," suggesting that this show of waywardness is but the mask of a profounder disaffection.

Tennyson dons a different mask in the burlesque "What Thor Said to the Bard before Dinner" (*UEP*). One recent commentator takes this poem as a straight-forward expression of the poet's determination "to write unhesitatingly of the abuses of the age and thus gain recognition."[6] The hobbledehoy manner, however, must surely have been intended as a caricature—though not therefore an absolute rejection—of all urgings to enlist his art in the public cause: "Spare not king or duke or critic,/Dealing out cross-buttock and flanker/With thy clanging analytic!" Tennyson makes Thor sound like a comic-strip Carlyle, and it is hard to suppose such an effect was inadvertent:

> Be not fairspoken neither stammer,
> Nail her, knuckle her, thou swinge-buckler!
> Spare not: ribroast gaffer and gammer,
> Be no shuffler, wear no muffler,
> But on thine anvil hammer and hammer!

Resistance to the idea of a more topical, more morally engaged art took other forms. Tennyson tells the sleeping beauty legend in "The Day-Dream," and in a section designated "Moral" says of the tale that it would "cramp its use" to "hook it to some useful end." "And is there any moral shut/Within the bosom of the rose?" he asks; and, when this response does not satisfy the pretended damsel to whom he tells the story, he grows playful and evasive and protests that it has its highest meaning as a compliment to her beauty. But Tennyson was still more inclined to treat the problem covertly. "The Hesperides," published in 1833 and then suppressed (it is significant how many of the poems that tend to stress the privacy of art were either unpublished or withdrawn), is among his most interesting symbolic expressions of the necessity for art somehow to keep "life" at a distance.[7]

The main part of the poem consists of a song sung by the daughters of Hesperus as they dance about the charmed tree where grows "the golden apple, the hallowed fruit." It is an incantation whose object is the protection of the apple, "the treasure/Of the wisdom of the West." As the singing preserves the magic fruit—"If ye sing not, if ye make false measure,/We shall lose eternal pleasure"—so the fruit is essential to the singers: "If the golden apple be taken/The world will be overwise." Adumbrated here is the mutual dependence of the poet's song and the secret wisdom that engenders it and is in turn perpetuated by it. The secret, however, is constantly imperiled: the apples must be guarded "Lest one from the East come and take it away." The West is associated with evening, the sea, fruition, and cunning;

the East, with morning, the land, spoliation, and bold strength. The two worlds are inimical and antagonistic: "Hesper hateth Phosphor, evening hateth morn." There is no doubt that the island paradise with its enchanted tree is preferable to all that threatens it ("All good things are in the west") and that in its separateness from "the world" lies the blessing of its preservation: "The world is wasted with fire and sword,/But the apple of gold hangs over the sea."

The violation of that separateness and its consequences are the subject of "The Lady of Shalott," a narrative poem but one that fits naturally among the works we are discussing. The antithetical realms are represented by Camelot and Sir Lancelot, on the one hand, and by Shalott and the unfortunate Lady, on the other. Camelot is the seat of heroic glory, of worldly activity, of human commerce. Shalott represents an obvious contrast; a "remote" island with wall and garden, it has the features commonly associated in Tennyson's poetry with the secluded and idyllic life of art. Night and day the Lady weaves "a magic web of colors gay," looking through a mirror at the "shadows of the world"—the reflection of the river and the high road that lead to Camelot. Like Plato's poet, she is an imitator of imitations; but his shadows were of the Ideal, hers are of the Actual. Fear of a curse keeps her from looking directly out upon the world; so, as the Hesperides guard their apple and preserve their paradise by continuous song, the Lady of Shalott keeps free of an unknown peril by steadily tending her loom with "little other care." Some of the sights her mirror reveals, especially a glimpse of human life, make the Lady long for the world of experience: "I am half sick of shadows." But the gay song and the dazzling reflection of Sir Lancelot are her undoing. He fairly epitomizes, with coal black curls, his sleek charger, and his glittering and jangling gear, the seductive appeal of "the world" to her lonely asceticism. When the Lady turns to behold him directly, the web unravels and the mirror cracks.

The conclusion is more effective as parable than as pathetic incident. The dying Lady's journey down the river to Camelot is her exhibition to the world of the sacrifice she has made for it. Like most public gestures made by retiring people, it does not quite hit the mark. Her swan song is ended as the boat passes under the city's tower, and the meaning of this mute tableau is too cryptic for the startled burghers. Puzzlement and fear are their only responses. But Lancelot's reaction gives the poem its crowning parabolic touch. He muses "a little space" upon the enigma of the maiden and then ventures the ultimate in fatuous blandness: "She has a lovely face." Such smug insensitivity throws into starkly ironic relief the futility as well as the fatality of the Lady's distraction from her craft or sullen art.

It is significant that, when Tennyson is possessed by a sense of the artist's moral duty, he resorts to allegory; in taking a more subversive line, he deals in the less direct strategies of symbol ("The Hesperides") and parable ("The Lady of Shalott"). One such allegory, a fragment written at Cambridge that reflects the arguments of his fellow Apostles, delineates the struggle between "Sense and Conscience" (*UEP*)—a clear anticipation of the moral meaning Tennyson was to assign his *Idylls of the King:* "Sense at war with Soul." The poem tells, awkwardly but primly, of the poet's "high Treason" in placing Sense in the seat of authority. Conscience, the else unconquerable champion, who seeks to free him from this thralldom, is stealthily drugged to sleep. Tennyson always had difficulty making such torpors seem sinister; the plight of Conscience suggests "The Lotos-Eaters," not to mention a famous purple patch in *The Princess:*

> A gloom monotonously musical
> With hum of murmurous bees, which brooded deep
> In ever-trembling flowers, and constant moan
> Of waterfalls i' th' distance, and low winds
> Wandering close to Earth, and voice of doves,
> Which ever bowing cooed and cooing bowed
> Unto each other as they could not cease.

This state is far from the Dionysian nightmare of Thomas Mann's *Death in Venice,* nor does it at all resemble the aphrodisiac torments of Tennyson's own "Lucretius"; but, nevertheless, the meaning is similar. The artist, "Lord of the senses five" as Tennyson calls him,[8] becomes their victim. Conscience is lulled by the poet's particular stock in trade: "dreams," "melodies," and "witching fantasies." A visitation from Memory only adds tears and sighs to his impotence. Finally, however, Conscience seizes his sword in rage and lays waste the garden that imprisons him. What in such poems as "The Poet's Mind" and "The Hesperides" symbolizes the earthly paradise of Art is here, of course, a second growth of Edmund Spenser's Bower of Bliss; and its just fate is the same as it is in the *Faerie Queene*. Yet, curiously, at this triumph of the Good over the Beautiful, there is a kind of revulsion. Such moral ambiguity is not rare in Tennyson's poetry.

It is certainly not absent from "The Palace of Art," a much more thoroughly rendered allegory for which "Sense and Conscience" might almost be a preliminary study. The poem was prefaced by dedicatory lines to Trench in which Tennyson describes the work as "a sort of allegory . . . of . . . A sinful soul possessed of many gifts . . . that did love beauty only" and declares that "he that shuts Love out, in turn shall be/Shut out from Love." The poem itself, then, would seem to be a sermon on Trench's Apostolic text, "we cannot live in art." But readers of the poem usually notice that Tennyson's heart seems less in his preaching than in his word painting.[9] Certainly the many scenes depicted on the arras which Tennyson drapes about his palace are very beautiful. And this is a good place to note how *picturesque*—how *poised*—Tennyson's descriptions typically are at their best; indeed, in such compositions of an arrested scene as the following, one sees what it was the Pre-Raphaelites found to learn from Tennyson:

> Or sweet Europa's mantle blew unclasp'd,
> From off her shoulder backward borne;
> From one hand droop'd a crocus; one hand grasp'd
> The mild bull's golden horn.

In this "lordly pleasure-house" that the poet builds for his soul we recognize many of the features Tennyson attached to the world of art in other poems: the fountain, an enclosed garden, and the emphasis upon both luxury and protection. Beyond all else, here the soul may "live alone unto herself"; she reigns apart in self-indulgence and unconcern for the world: "All these are mine,/And let the world have peace or wars,/'Tis one to me." Underlying the artist-soul's separation and self-sufficiency is the crucial metaphor: the artist is God.

James Joyce's Stephen Dedalus has evoked for us the vivid picture of "the artist, like the God of the creation . . . indifferent, paring his fingernails." Tennyson's "soul" is no less indifferent in her "Godlike isolation." She is also like a deity in her absolute dominion: "Lord over Nature, lord of the visible earth,/Lord of the senses five." Moreover, to create as the artist-soul does is "to mimic heaven." Even her lack of intellectual commitment is a sign of the soul's divinity: "I sit as God holding no form of creed,/But contemplating all." Thus the poem exhibits the ultimate perversion of the honored tradition, which Tennyson elsewhere affirms, of the poet as divine voice. The poet-prophet, however, is the instrument of God; the poet-magician in exalting himself above his kind and arrogating to himself divine powers commits a foolish blasphemy.

Retribution, when it comes, has an ironic fitness: the soul who had gloried in her "Godlike isolation" now feels "exiled from eternal God." However, the transformation of the palace into a charnel house is not merely a punishment but, we are told, a providential means of effecting the soul's redemption:

> Lest she should fail and perish utterly,
> God, before whom ever lie bare
> The abysmal deeps of personality,
> Plagued her with sore despair.

But this is not, in fact, either the most insistent or the most interesting aspect of the poem's reversal. The impression given is not so much that of a divine visitation as it is of an *internal,* self-generated corruption:

> A spot of dull stagnation, without light
> Or power of movement, seem'd my soul.
> . . . .
> Back on herself her serpent pride had curl'd.
> . . . .
> She, mouldering with the dull earth's mouldering sod,
> Inwrapt tenfold in slothful shame. . . .

Such descriptions of the nausea of self-confrontation suggest that the soul's calamity in "The Palace of Art" offers more as psychological insight than as moral pronouncement. The equivocal conclusion—wherein the soul, though retreating to a simple cottage to "mourn and pray," hopes someday to return to the palace, "So lightly, beautifully built"—supports this view. As Trench had told Tennyson, "We cannot live in art"; but that is only because the soul is somehow unfit to live in it. Tennyson's morbidity made guilt a more or less natural feeling, but his artist's pride would not let him condemn his handiwork.

With "The Palace of Art" Tennyson virtually closed the debate with himself as to whether the poet's mind was a private sanctuary or a public oracle. He came to have less and less sympathy for estheticism and wrote a mocking epigram on "Art for Art's sake (instead of Art for Art—and—Man's sake)." [10] Yet, as we shall see, the problem does recur in *In Memoriam* and finally was abandoned rather than resolved. Though the Tennyson of the later years was assuredly the responsible Laureate and not the idle singer of an empty day, he did not quite become that charismatic figure he envisioned in "The Poet": there was not the ardor of clear commitment. Thus the debate is more than the subject, in one way or another, of many of Tennyson's early poems; it underlies what seems a persistent vacillation in his lyric art. This vacillation—strange in a poet so skilled with language—is between two manners which may be called "declarative" and "evocative." Either of these manners would have benefited from some of the qualities of the other, but Tennyson did not consistently manage a satisfactory fusion.

One of Matthew Arnold's letters to his sister complains of "the modern English habit . . . of using poetry as a channel for thinking aloud, instead of making anything." [11] Much of Tennyson's lyric verse—when he is not being elaborately tuneful—gives just this impression. Perhaps he mistakes sincerity for lyrical invention; in the poem "Isabel," a tribute to his mother, we encounter such utterly flavorless passages as this: "The intuitive decision of a bright/And thorough-edged intellect to part/Error from crime . . ." More typical is the versified thought of poems like "By an Evolutionist": "If my body come from brutes, tho' somewhat finer than their own,/I am heir, and this my kingdom. Shall the royal voice be mute?"—or "The Higher Pantheism": "Dark is the world to thee; thyself art the reason why,/For is He not all but thou, that hast power to feel 'I am I'?"

"The Ancient Sage" virtually symbolizes this tendency to unstring the lyre and to prose on under the homiletic compulsion. Reading from a scroll the verses of a young skeptic, the sage breaks in upon himself to offer moral advice to the author of the verses (who, one is tempted to suppose, seeks not a sermon but literary criticism):

For nothing worthy proving can be proven,
Nor yet disproven. Wherefore thou be wise,
Cleave ever to the sunnier side of doubt,
And cling to Faith beyond the forms of Faith!

With its paradoxes marked by the disagreeable smugness of pseudo-profundity, such utterance is unredeemed even by the wit or verbal crispness of aphorism.

As examples of the evocative manner, which does not make statements about life but rather, as Marianne Moore phrases it, "presents for our inspection" objects of the poet's vision, we might cite two strikingly dissimilar poems that, each in its own way, call worlds into being. "The Kraken" is the awesome evocation of that fabulous sea monster in his secret life at the bottom of the deep. The creature's enormity, the profundity and weirdness of his abode, and his utter absorption in "ancient, dreamless, uninvaded sleep"—all of which the poem superbly captures—imbue him with an enigmatic power.

Only when the holocaust of the world's end heats the depths of the ocean will the Kraken breach to astound both man and angels with the sight: "In roaring he shall rise and on the surface die." An impressive feat of the imagination, it is as disquieting and phantasmagoric in its way as the advent of Yeats's Sphinx in his "Second Coming." But, whereas Yeats's beast is a brilliant elucidation, the import of Tennyson's image is vague. Not every reader would see this vagueness as a fault; it may be enough that Tennyson has depicted the Kraken so memorably. And yet the poem surely invites us to regard the monster as somehow portentous, while it provides no real clue as to what it portends.

In "Sir Launcelot and Queen Guinevere" Tennyson renders with exquisite detail that springtime moment when all the world trembles with new life:

In crystal vapour everywhere
Blue isles of heaven laugh'd between,
And far, in forest-deeps unseen,
The topmost elm-tree gather'd green
From draughts of balmy air.

Into this verdant beauty ride the young knight and the new queen, perfect players in such a scene for romance. The whole poem is redolent with the freshness and wonder of first love. We know, of course, the sorry outcome of that legendary amour, but Tennyson handles his subject in such a way that this knowledge casts not the pall of irony but the glint of poignancy upon this early episode:

> She look'd so lovely as she sway'd
> The rein with dainty finger-tips,
> A man had given all other bliss,
> And all his worldly worth for this,
> To waste his whole heart in one kiss
> Upon her perfect lips.

Good as the poem is, it virtually flaunts its lack of consequence, as Tennyson may have sensed when he published the poem as "a fragment." [12] It is a case of Tennyson's diffidence; just as, at one extreme, his blatant moralizing results from his unwillingness to subject his thought to the pressures of fancy, so, at the other, timidity again prevents him in a poem like this from transforming what he can imagine into something it is important to express. The instinct that tempted Tennyson the poet to shun the world was only in part a desire to keep his art intact; deeper still, one feels, lay a suspicion that his poetic vision was unequal to the comprehension and encompassment of life in its broader and more complex ranges.

W. H. Auden has very perceptively noted that Tennyson's poems "deal with human emotions in their most primitive states." [13] This statement is particularly true in the sense that his best poems—poems that seem, as it were, to engage the "whole poet"—reiterate only a few fundamental, intellectually unsophisticated attitudes. Indeed, one of these, a longing for the "lost and gone," virtually subsumes the others and gives the dominant key to Tennyson's lyric strain.

III *The Passion of the Past* [14]

In a passage from "The Ancient Sage" which Tennyson singled out as particularly expressive of his personal feelings,[15] he characterizes a vague but powerful fascination that the past held for him:

. . . oft
On me, when boy, there came what then I call'd,
Who knew no books and no philosophies,
In my boy-phrase, 'The Passion of the Past.'
The first gray streak of earliest summer-dawn,
The last long strife of waning crimson gloom,
As if the late and early were but one—
A height, a broken grange, a grove, a flower
Had murmurs, 'Lost and gone, and lost and gone!'
A breath, a whisper—some divine farewell—
Desolate sweetness—far and far away—
What had he loved, what had he lost, the boy?
I know not, and I speak of what has been.

The relation of this passion of the past to Tennyson's poetic impulse suggests that it can be understood neither as a mere romantic commonplace nor as the simple reflection of personal experience. Both these elements are, of course, involved; a longing for the snows of yesteryear would have seemed an inevitable topic to any poet brought up on such preterists as Thomas Moore and Walter Scott, not to mention Virgil, and a moving one indeed to the poet whose boy's heart had broken at the news, "Byron is dead!" But Tennyson's feeling about the past goes beyond literary tradition, and it goes also beyond regret at a specific loss or a desire to relive a particular experience: his is an almost metaphysical apprehension concerning the past in its relation to meaningful existence. "It is the distance that charms me in the landscape, the picture and the past," Tennyson told Sir James Knowles;[16] and in *In Memoriam* he admitted that "the past will always win/A glory from its being far" (XXIV). Not *a* past, not something *in* the past, but "pastness" itself was the essential object of his longing and thus the ultimate burden of his song.

Fundamental to the Tennysonian *Sehnsucht* was what James Spedding described as his friend's "almost personal dislike of the present."[17] The quality that, for Tennyson, characterized the present was its emptiness; hence his aversion to it is experienced more in numbness than in anguish. Present existence is a vacuity where nothing can be really *felt*, not even pain in the usual sense. In "Perdidi Diem" (*UEP*) the young poet laments: "I never *liv'd* a day, but daily die,/I have no real breath;/My being is a vacant worthlessness." Containing no quality to which emotions may attach themselves, the present has neither meaning nor essential reality. "To me," Tennyson once wrote Emily Sellwood, "often the far-off world seems nearer than the present, for in the present is always something unreal and indistinct, but the other seems a good solid planet, rolling round its green hills and paradises to the harmony of more steadfast laws." [18] In contrast to the empty unreality of the present, then, the past—that "good, solid planet"—appealed to Tennyson especially because of its plenitude and stable permanence.

His earliest poems abound in images of present ruin, reminders of a richer past. In one of the most suggestive of these, "The Old Sword" (*Poems by Two Brothers*), that "wreck of ancient time," corroded and useless but a memorial to intense and glorious existence, becomes the veritable emblem of Tennyson's sense of impotence and nostalgia. The human situations with which Tennyson's poems are most characteristically concerned also express this longing of the empty present for the fullness of the past: situations of abandonment, exile, or—naturally enough, considering his father's financial misfortune—disinheritance.

In poems like "Mariana" and "Mariana in the South" Tennyson exhibits his unique powers of rendering the atmosphere of desolation: both works present forlorn ladies lamenting their abandonment. However, the lament itself, which is in each poem borne largely by a refrain, is not the chief means of expressing the desolate mood; the scenic descriptions brilliantly perform that function. In "Mariana" the scene is evoked at different moments in the day, but the emphasis is upon its unvarying dreariness:

> With blackest moss the flower-plots
> Were thickly crusted, one and all;
> The rusted nails fell from the knots
> That held the pear to the gable-wall.
> The broken sheds look'd sad and strange:
>   Unlifted was the clinking latch;
>   Weeded and worn the ancient thatch
> Upon the lonely moated grange.

This present is rendered as monotonous and attenuated temporality; the crusted moss, the rusted nails, the broken sheds, and—in other stanzas—the swaying of a gusty shadow, the creaking of doors, and the slow ticking of a clock all suggest the wearing away of time without fulfillment. Small sounds that only deepen the human silence echo the emptiness of hopeless and tedious existence: the buzz of flies, the chirp of a sparrow, the moaning of the wind.

The companion piece, "Mariana in the South," achieves an atmosphere of almost equally unendurable vacancy in a scene dominated by stifling heat, choking dust, numbing silence:

With one black shadow at its feet,
The house thro' all the level shines,
Close-latticed to the brooding heat,
And silent in its dusty vines;
A faint-blue ridge upon the right,
An empty river-bed before,
And shallows on a distant shore,
In glaring sand and inlets bright.

Brief quotation can hardly suggest the extraordinary success of both poems in conveying the state of internal desolation. "Mariana" must be considered the more impressive if for no other reason than that the "physical exterior" objectifies the "emotional interior" without any explicit connection between these two dimensions of the poem having to be asserted. But each poem is the kind of performance John Stuart Mill had in mind when he distinguished Tennyson's descriptive poetry from "that rather vapid species of composition" usually designated by the phrase. Mill speaks of Tennyson's "power of *creating* scenery, in keeping with some state of human feeling so fitted to it as to be the embodied symbol of it, and to summon up the state of feeling itself, with a force not to be surpassed by anything but reality." [19]

In Time there is no present,
In eternity no future,
In eternity no past.
("The 'How' and the 'Why' ")

Tennyson's disregard for the present and his passion for the past reflect his awareness of the inherent pathos of self-conscious temporal existence. Unlike eternity, in which all things would perforce be present, time has "no present," so evanescent is that dimensionless point we call *now*. Awareness has reference to what has already been experienced or can be anticipated. Thus, those who live in hope do not mourn the past; for them, time is fulfillment, not distance or deprivation; and the present is a vital link in meaningful process. In the idyllic world of "The Miller's Daughter," "Past and Present, wound in one,/Do make a garland for the heart," but with disillusionment or bereavement comes a rending of this almost prelapsarian sense of temporal continuity.

Poem after poem echoes with what Tennyson, in "Locksley Hall," terms "the 'Never, never,' whisper'd by the phantom years." The mood finds its distillation in such a lyric as "Break, break, break," whose very economy of means gives admirable precision and intensity to Tennyson's overwhelming sense of transience:

> Break, break, break,
> On thy cold gray stones, O Sea!
> And I would that my tongue could utter
> The thoughts that arise in me.
>
> O, well for the fisherman's boy,
> That he shouts with his sister at play!
> O, well for the sailor lad,
> That he sings in his boat on the bay!
>
> And the stately ships go on
> To their haven under the hill;
> But O for the touch of a vanish'd hand,
> And the sound of a voice that is still!
>
> Break, break, break,
> At the foot of thy crags, O Sea!
> But the tender grace of a day that is dead
> Will never come back to me.

The controlling impression of inner desolation surrounded by indifference is achieved mainly by the contrast between the grieving lyrical "I" and those objects in the poem—the sea, the fisherman's boy, the sailor lad, and the stately ships—that are oblivious to him and unaffected by his grief. More decisive still is the relationship of these elements to the dominating image of the sea. Its rhythmic crash suggests the relentless surge of time itself. The other characters of the poem are inseparably involved with the sea; it is, so to say, their natural element.

Images richly and variously suggestive of a harmony with temporal existence are arranged to suggest as well the increasing involvement in that existence from childhood to youth to maturity (the playing along the shore, the sailing in the bay, the completion of a voyage on the sea). In contrast is the isolation of the poet, who may see in the innocence and promise of youth and in the close of a prosperous voyage cause for joy but who cannot share it. The shouting and the singing are pointed opposites of the "stilled voice" of the loved one and of the poet's own unutterable sorrow; the ships' anticipated homecoming is the emotional antithesis of the mourner's longing for the vanished hand.

Even the vagueness of the poet's grief has a special aptness. We readily infer the death of a loved one, but the poem is bare of details in that respect. In the final stanza the reference to "a day that is dead" associates death with the passage of time and has the effect of enlarging or generalizing the theme, while at the same time giving it a more distinctive emotional resonance. For ultimately it is not merely the vanished hand, nor, for that matter, the dead day itself that the poet mourns; time does not stand still, even for the fisherman's boy and the sailor lad. The keenest loss is the ability to recapture that day's tender grace, a grace—manifest in the boy and the lad—through which time seems to lead toward rather than away from the heart's desire. The poem thus becomes more than a personal lament; it is made an expression of the universal tragedy of temporal existence.

But this tragic awareness does not prevent Tennyson from seeking various means of establishing some kind of connection with the past and the values inherent in it. One very direct way that becomes the subject of several poems is through actual revisitation of scenes from the personal past—as if the efficacy of *place* might regain what *time* has taken. Ironically, of course, such returns may not nullify what Tennyson calls "the curse of time" but actually intensify it. So in one of the *Poems by Two Brothers*, "The Dell of E——," the poet is stunned by the contrast between the fresh, virginal haunt of his youth and the dell as it is after "man's rude hand had sorely scath'd" it. However, this poem is only partially a lament for the passing of time as such; it is primarily a conventional protest against the ravages of an industrial civilization. Yet even without the impression of physical change, a return can bring with it more of a sense of separation from the past than a recovery of it. Thus in verses on Mablethorpe,[20] the seacoast retreat of Tennyson's childhood, the poet records no outward transformation; it is the oppressive actuality of the place that disillusions him:

> And here again I come, and only find
>   The drain-cut level of the marshy lea,
> Gray sand-banks, and pale sunsets, dreary wind,
>   Dim shores, dense rains, and heavy-clouded sea.

He regains *only* the reality of sensation; he cannot recapture that tender grace by which such a scene had been "the infant Ilion of the mind."

In his later, less melancholy moods, Tennyson could find in physical return something of a compensation for the passage of the years. He revisited in 1861 a valley in the Pyrenees where he had been with Arthur Hallam more than thirty years before. The experience—or so the poem "In the Valley of Cauteretz" affirms—virtually expunged the interval and effected a kind of mystical reunion with his dead friend:

> All along the valley, while I walk'd today,
> The two and thirty years were a mist that rolls away;
> . . . .
> And all along the valley, by rock and cave and tree,
> The voice of the dead was a living voice to me.

Less mystical, but engagingly personal, is the very old poet's gallant tribute to his youthful infatuation for Rosa Baring, a beauty of the Somersby neighborhood:

> Rose, on this terrace fifty years ago,
>   When I was in my June, you in your May
> Two words, '*My* Rose,' set all your face aglow,
>   And now that I am white and you are gray,
> That blush of fifty years ago, my dear,
>   Blooms in the past, but close to me to-day,
> As this red rose, which on our terrace here
>   Glows in the blue of fifty miles away.
>
> ("The Roses on the Terrace")

Interesting here is the explicit analogy between the dimensions of time and space, suggesting, at least to the mellowness of age, that distances do not separate absolutely.

For there is, after all, memory: the faculty that sustains the imagination in the dreary present, keeping contact with the substance and vitality that seems to reside only in the past:

> The Present is the vassal of the Past:
> So that, in that I *have* lived, do I live,
> And cannot die, and am, in having been—
> A portion of the pleasant yesterday,
> Thrust forward on to-day and out of place;
> A body journeying onward, sick with toil,
> The weight as if of age upon my limbs,
> The grasp of hopeless grief about my heart,
> And all the senses weaken'd, save in that,
> Which long ago they had glean'd and garner'd up
> Into the granaries of memory.
> (*The Lover's Tale*, ll. 115–25)

Three of Tennyson's early poems are invocations to Memory. They prove his interest in that faculty as a means of access to the wellsprings of poetry, but they also attest to the inherent ambivalence of Tennyson's attitude toward its powers. The "Ode to Memory" (1830) is the most affirmative of the three poems, ecstatically celebrating, in somewhat mixed images, memory's Promethean gift:

> Thou who stealest fire,
> From the fountains of the past,
> To glorify the present, O, haste,
> Visit my low desire!

There is the suggestion that memory sometimes brings with it melancholy, but the burden of the work is the poet's expectation of rapturous enlightenment. More particularly, memory is looked to paradoxically as the source of hope for the future: "In sweet dreams softer than unbroken rest/Thou leddest by the hand thine infant Hope. . . ." This relationship between memory and hope also occurs in a fragment "Memory" (*UEP*). The poem introduces the concept in almost identical terms—". . . Hope is born of

Memory/Nightly in the house of dreams"—pursuing it, however, to a much less consoling insight: "But when I wake, at once she seems/The faery changeling wan Despair." This poem, in fact, addresses a "Blessèd, cursèd, Memory" whose visions of past felicity can ultimately serve only as a mockery of the present. To succumb to the appeal of memory is to exacerbate the sense of desolation: "O dark of bright! O foul of fair!"

Poems by Two Brothers included another "Memory," a more tepid poem perhaps, but one similarly imbued with this double sense of attraction and repulsion. The fragment envisions memory as a grim specter who haunts the poet "From the body of the Past,/Like a wandering ghost aghast." This other "Memory" speaks more mildly of a "dear enchanter" and of recollections as promising blooms that fell from the tree before they could grow into ripe fruit. Both poems agree on the ironic fact, noted by Dante, whom Tennyson paraphrased in "Locksley Hall," "That a sorrow's crown of sorrow is remembering happier things."

Whether "dear enchanter" or "wandering ghost," memory practices an uncanny art upon the present, and yet the imagination does not thereby possess the past but is possessed by it. The difference is crucial, underlying as it does the distinctive poignancy of Tennyson's passion for the past. Without question, the key text is the most consistently admired of all Tennyson's lyrics: "Tears, idle tears," one of the blank verse songs in *The Princess.* "Once read," said Andrew Lang, "it seems like a thing that has always existed in the world of poetic archetypes": [21]

> Tears, idle tears, I know not what they mean,
> Tears from the depth of some divine despair
> Rise in the heart, and gather to the eyes,
> In looking on the happy autumn-fields,
> And thinking of the days that are no more.
>
> Fresh as the first beam glittering on a sail,
> That brings our friends up from the underworld,
> Sad as the last which reddens over one
> That sinks with all we love below the verge;
> So sad, so fresh, the days that are no more.
>
> Ah, sad and strange as in dark summer dawns
> The earliest pipe of half-awaken'd birds

To dying ears, when unto dying eyes
The casement slowly grows a glimmering square;
So sad, so strange, the days that are no more.

Dear as remember'd kisses after death,
And sweet as those by hopeless fancy feign'd
On lips that are for others; deep as love,
Deep as first love, and wild with all regret;
O Death in Life, the days that are no more!

Tennyson has recorded that he wrote this poem at Tintern Abbey, "full for me of its bygone memories." [22] These memories, however, seem to have been of a less definite and personal kind than those which moved Wordsworth to write that other great memory poem that was composed a few miles away. A comparison of the two works is revealing; there is in Tennyson's poem none of his predecessor's serene confidence that the "wild ecstasies" of the past "shall be matured/Into a sober pleasure" and that memory is but "a dwelling place/For all sweet sounds and harmonies." [23] Wordsworth's poem celebrates the communion of man and nature, and it reaffirms meaningful existence by asserting the essential continuity of human experience. "Tears, idle tears," on the other hand, perhaps typifying a later stage of the Romantic sensibility,[24] is permeated by the feeling of alienation and discontinuity.

Tennyson's testimony that the occasion of the poem was "not real woe" [25] is of course, no reflection upon the genuineness of the emotion; but it does suggest that the tears have no specific cause. In that sense, they are *idle;* their source can only be identified as "some divine despair," some transcendent sorrow of which individual grief is but a particular embodiment. These are the *lacrimae rerum,* the tears for things that have receded into the past. But, if the poet's is a general sorrow at the temporal process, the immediate occasion is his sight of "happy" autumn fields. The situation is similar in some respects to that in "Break, break, break"; the autumn fields, "happy" in the sense they represent fulfillment, bring home to the weeper by the force of contrast his own deprivation.

Moreover, this disparity between the plenitude of external nature and the desolation of the conscious self signals a rupture within that consciousness. For the poem is concerned, fundamentally, with the emotional dilemma implied by the dramatic contrast between *looking* on the happy autumn-fields and *thinking* of the days that are no more. Sensation and reflection are disconnected, or if there is a relationship it is an ironic one in which the perception of "happiness" evokes sorrow in the percipient. Here, feeling does not come in aid of feeling, as for Wordsworth; nor does Tennyson recognize, as does Wordsworth,

> In nature and the language of the sense,
> The anchor of my purest thoughts, the nurse,
> The guide, the guardian of my heart, and soul
> Of all my mortal being.
> ("Tintern Abbey," ll. 108–11)

Thus Tennyson's autumn fields are neither an aid to reflection nor an alternative to it; they merely drop from view as the poet pursues his feelings about bygone days. And this effort of memory, though resulting from the inadequacy of the present, cannot quite attain the immediacy of sensation and so fails as an attempt to recover the past.

The complexity of Tennyson's attitude towards memory and the past informs virtually every detail of the poem as the strangeness of the past is delicately balanced against its familiarity. The past, as Tennyson writes elsewhere, "is like a travell'd land now sunk/Below the horizon" (*The Cup,* II, 134–135). Thus in "Tears, idle tears," the ship returning from the underworld and the one sinking below the verge are associated with the unknown realms; but they bear with them "friends" and "all we love." Finally, the epithet *wild,* though applied to his memories, seems borrowed from the present mood of the mourner himself, who is frantic in his regret. This transference has a special appropriateness to Tennyson's conception of the past. Just as the idle tears express personal feeling yet originate, as it were, in some supra-personal source, there is a passion, a stirring, that inheres both in the past itself and in him who longs for it. The ambiguity of Tennyson's own phrase, "the Passion *of* the Past," expresses this double sense of desire *for* the days that are no more, on the one hand, and, on the other, the almost autonomous life these days assume within the memory.

Yet, for all the seeming vitality of the days, they are a "death in life" and no real imaginative escape from the barren present.

Some of Tennyson's poems examine other alternatives, particularly the worlds of dream and trance and of myth or legend; they too hold the promise of a life out of time in which "the tender grace of a day that is dead" might be recaptured or simulated. From earliest childhood Tennyson placed a special value upon the trance-like state induced, it seems, by the aura of a certain word or phrase. His own name could produce this mystical effect, as "The Ancient Sage" reveals:

more than once when I
Sat all alone, revolving in myself
The word that is the symbol of myself,
The mortal limit of the Self was loosed,
And passed into the Nameless, as a cloud
Melts into heaven.

The poem "Far—far—away" treats the "strange charm" [26] these words always had for Tennyson, a "vague-world whisper," as the poem calls it, from the dawn of life and beyond the bounds of temporal experience. And in an early sonnet that commemorates his first meeting with Hallam, Tennyson describes a mood of abstraction in which

we muse and brood,
And ebb into a former life, or seem
To lapse far back in some confused dream
To states of mystical similitude.
("To ——")

The boyhood poem, "Armageddon," is built around a considerably embellished but essentially similar ecstasy: "All sense of Time/And Being and Place was swallowed up and lost/Within a victory of boundless thought" (*UEP*).

Tennyson ascribed much the same appeal to what he termed "delicious dreams, our other life." [27] Several of his poems are in the dream-vision tradition: "A Dream of Fair Women," "The Day-Dream," and "The Vision of Sin" are examples. And dreams figure importantly in other poems, as in the conclusion of "Morte d'Arthur," where Everard Hall's epic recital prompts the narrator to dream of "King Arthur, like a modern gentleman"; but we are concerned at present more with a lyric brooding upon dreams than with their function in narrative. Tennyson imagines sleep as a release of the soul from its temporal bonds and dreams as a means of reunion with the past:

> Sleep, Death's twin-brother, knows not Death,
> Nor can I dream of thee as dead.
>
> I walk as ere I walk'd forlorn,
> When all our path was fresh with dew . . .
> (*In Memoriam*, LXVIII)

As Tennyson acknowledges in a subsequent lyric, dreams may be troubled; but, when sleep can "Drug down the blindfold sense of wrong," the pleasure of dreams "may be whole," unattended by the painful consciousness of the present that accompanies memory. To the dreamer, the temporal dimension is absent while sleep forges "a night-long present of the past" (*In Memoriam*, LXXI). Nor is this renewal mere illusion; for, as Tennyson insists in "The Higher Pantheism," "Dreams are true while they last, and do we not live in dreams?"

The dream life, though real in its way, is sporadic and intractable; and Tennyson sees that, as a link to the past, such a life is therefore obviously limited. "In Deep and Solemn Dreams" (*UEP*), one of his first dream poems, is concerned with both the appeal and the ultimate inadequacy of the dream state. It describes the dream world as a City of the Blest, "Brooded o'er by dovelike rest" whose perfect stasis involves a recovery of the past:

> All adown the busy ways
> Come sunny faces of lost days,
> Long to mouldering dust consign'd,
> Forms which live but in the mind.

These faces look upon the poet "With tearless ageless eyes," and the poem later refers to "The sacred charm of tearless sleep"; it is significant that such dreams are thus free of the "idle tears" that inevitably attend temporal memory. The dream, however, cannot last; it fades away, leaving the poet "Hopeless, heartless and forlorn." This evanescence is the theme of another early poem, "And ask ye why these sad tears stream," in which the poet dreams of his beloved "as 't was yesterday"; but the vision vanishes, and he awakens "doubly weary." The dreamer may re-experience the past; but, because the dream is independent of his will, he can neither retain nor recall it. In "A Dream of Fair Women" Tennyson expressly likens the futile attempt to recover a dream to the vain efforts of memory. As their appeal to the nostalgic imagination is similar, so memory and dream—though different in the nature of their success—are alike in their ultimate failure.

It was the realm of myths and legends that came closest to constituting an idealized past that could solace Tennyson's imagination as a kind of eternal presence. Memory, as Tennyson observed in "The Two Voices," deals but with time and so cannot enable the soul to "climb/Beyond her own material prime" (ll. 377–78); dreams are only "true while they last." But myths are like King Arthur's city: "built/To music, therefore never built at all,/And therefore built forever." [28] "The Lotos-Eaters," one of the crucial poems of Tennyson's early maturity, provides a particularly useful illustration of his deep affinity for "that new world which is the old." [29] A mythological poem having to do with the contrast between two antithetical kinds of existence, it itself represents one of these antitheses. The poem is not only *about* lotos-land; it is a product of the lotos-land of Tennyson's mythological imagination.

The most notable feature of this land of the lotos-eaters is its timelessness. It is "a land/In which it seemed always afternoon," "A land where all things always seem'd the same." Time stands still, and change and transience are unknown. In sharp contrast is the ceaseless motion of the desolate sea—"the wandering fields of barren foam"—on which Odysseus and his men have been wearisomely journeying. The sea thus represents, as it does in "Break, break, break," a temporal existence from which the lotos fruit offers escape into "dreamful ease." To one who has tasted the fruit, the breaking waves sound distant and meaningless:

> whoso did receive of them
> And taste, to him the gushing of the wave
> Far far away did seem to mourn and rave
> On alien shores.

This flight from time and toil is not, as in the Homeric original, mere oblivion. It is the attainment of a transcendent awareness; the enchanted branches of the lotos enable one "To muse and brood and live again in memory,/With those old faces of our infancy." Not only exempt from Time, this existence is also one in which the past can somehow be recovered. Tennyson uses the word *memory*, but the memories of the lotos-eaters are quite distinct from those ordinary temporal recollections which, though dear, are of the mutable and hence lack the compelling power: "Dear is the memory of our wedded lives,/And dear the last embraces of our wives/And their warm tears; but all hath suffer'd change." Whereas the one kind of "memory" can negate time, the other actually intensifies the mariners' painful sense of transience:

> Time driveth onward fast,
> And in a little while our lips are dumb.
> Let us alone. What is it that will last?
> All things are taken from us, and become
> Portions and parcels of the dreadful past.

As a realm beyond the reach of time, where the tender grace of the past is eternally present, the land of the lotos-eaters depicts an imaginative ideal which myth and legend could in their way realize. Arthur Hallam is mythicized into the dying king of "Morte d'Arthur"; Tennyson's own grief and resolution not to yield find their mythic translation in "Tithonus" and "Ulysses." In the way these and other mythic figures could objectify his own moods, he discovered an imaginative means by which the self might in some measure elude the isolation and flux of temporal existence. In so doing, it should be added, Tennyson was to that extent led away from the subjectivity of lyric into the more impersonal mode of narrative and dramatic (especially monologue) forms. And of course, given his particular qualities as an artist, this shift involved real loss as well as gain.

As for "The Lotos Eaters," no reader could feel that its dreamful ease was being presented as an unqualified ideal. The positive values of timelessness and contact with the past involve the forsaking of responsibility and an indifference to humanity; and, although this poem lacks the high moral tone Tennyson all too often took, we recognize it as another version of the "palace of art" theme. As he went on to explore the lotos-land of myth and legend, Tennyson tried conscientiously to relate it to timely human concerns. "It is no use," he told his son, "giving a mere *réchauffé* of old legends."[30] Consequently, it became his customary technique to cast such material in what he considered a modern "frame." Even treated in this way, the old legends remained one important source of that "far and far away" to which Tennyson was always responsive. The Laureate became increasingly involved with maintaining for his art a suitable place in "the march of mind"; but, as an Ancient Sage, he could still ask the question to which, early and late, he sought reply: "To-day? but what of yesterday?"

IV In Memoriam

In Memoriam, generally regarded as Tennyson's masterpiece, is probably the work upon which his claims as the major poet of the Victorian age must permanently rest. Certainly it is the capstone of his lyric art; each of the topics with which this chapter has thus far dealt finds a kind of culmination in *In Memoriam.* Its unvaried use of the distinctive four-line stanza puts Tennyson's mastery of rhythm and sound to an extreme test; in it, his divided sense of the poet's task is crucially evident; and it is his most elaborate descant upon his passion of the past.

Arthur Hallam, two years younger than Tennyson, entered Trinity College in 1828; and both young men were chosen to the society of the Apostles the following year. Son of the noted historian and a person gifted by nature and privileged in his upbringing, Hallam seemed to Tennyson and to many others destined for a life of great influence and achievement. In almost every respect he was the opposite of his diffident, melancholy, and rough-hewn friend. Cambridge was natural to Hallam; to Tennyson it was not. Under such circumstances, Alfred might have felt sufficiently fortunate merely to be included among Arthur's friends; but Hallam, who was half-hearted in nothing, took him up in a way that must have been overwhelming. Together they carried money to Spanish rebels in the Pyrenees and toured the Rhineland; a joint volume of their poems was projected; Hallam published an essay on modern poetry that eulogized *Poems, Chiefly Lyrical;* and, after the way of storied friendships, Hallam fell in love with Tennyson's sister, Emily, and they were engaged to be married.

Hallam's death in 1833 in Vienna during a Continental tour

with his father was a brutal shock. Suddenly, and from a strange place, a letter informed Tennyson that his friend was no more. This loss was the climactic event of Tennyson's emotional life. By it, the melancholy intimations that haunt his early poetry were confirmed in experience; a poetic attitude was transformed into a biographical fact.

Tennyson began recording his sorrow and commemorating his friend in brief "elegies," as he called them; and these accumulated for nearly seventeen years before they were published as *In Memoriam.* He did not conceive of them as a single work nor think of publishing them until most had been written. Their arrangement does not reflect the precise order of composition; and, though an after-thought, it is not merely haphazard; for Tennyson tried to suggest in the completed sequence something of the traditional elegiac movement from grief to consolation. Contemporary readers, who found the result heartening, valued the poem chiefly as a profession of faith in the face of personal bereavement and disquieting intellectual conflict. To modern readers, on the other hand, its interest lies largely in those sections that betray emotional vulnerability, confusion, and doubt—and thus suggest and in a measure speak for those levels of the Victorian consciousness beneath its surface optimism and complacency. It is a question of whether the reader is the more moved by the work's total pattern, which is essentially affirmative, or by the mood of deep perplexity and anguish that dominates many of its finest parts.

The looseness of the poem's structure and of its relation to the conventions of elegy is set off against an extreme rigidity of prosodic form. The one hundred and thirty-three separate lyrics that the work in its final form comprises total seven hundred and twenty-four stanzas, all made up of four tetrameter lines rhymed *a b b a.* The resulting monotony, which FitzGerald and many others have remarked, is less damaging than it might be; for stanzaic regularity gives an element of cohesion to what is otherwise an extremely diffuse work. Moreover, despite such restricted means, Tennyson draws from his "sad mechanic exercise" a considerable variety of effects. The poem encompasses a range of styles, from the simplicity of direct statement to the convolutions of statement and counterstatement, from the familiar and intimate to the elevated and formal. We read, for example, "I loved the weight I had to bear,/Because it needed help of Love . . ." (XXV) and also "Our wills are ours, we know not how;/Our wills are ours, to make them thine" (Prologue).

The shifting emotions that the poem records are contained within the unvaried frame by Tennyson's fine ear and by his ability to modulate rhythms to catch the mood of the occasion:

Calm on the seas, and silver sleep,
And waves that sway themselves in rest,
And dead calm in that noble breast
Which heaves but with the heaving deep.
(XI)

. . . .

Ring out the old, ring in the new,
Ring, happy bells, across the snow:
The year is going, let him go;
Ring out the false, ring in the true.
(CVI)

Besides the virtuosity with which Tennyson manipulates it, the stanza form he chose has its own peculiar appropriateness. It is not too fanciful to assert a correspondence, or at least an affinity, between the movement of the *In Memoriam* stanza and the characteristic movements of feeling and thought in the poem. In Canto XLVIII Tennyson refers depreciatively to these lyrics as "Short swallow-flights of song, that dip/Their wings in tears, and skim away." The description is remarkably apt; again and again single poems describe a kind of reaching out toward some definitive expression of emotion, or some conclusive declaration of conviction; and then there is a flitting away, a lapsing of the moment of intensity. And, as this is a recurrent pattern in the separate lyrics, so is it surely the gesture implied by the individual stanza. The rhyme scheme takes us out, so to speak, suspends us in the stress of its interior couplet, then subsides, falling back upon the end sound of the initial line:

Who show'd a token of distress?
No single tear, no mark of pain—
O sorrow, then can sorrow wain?
O grief, can grief be changed to less?
(LXXVIII)

. . . .
O life as futile, then, as frail!
O for thy voice to soothe and bless!
What hope of answer or redress?
Behind the veil, behind the veil.
(LVI)

It is a gesture of futility, of frustration; and that is precisely the impression the poem most authentically conveys. Its thought is marked by tentativeness; its emotion is repeatedly being reined in. Even though such qualities may be, in themselves, a weakness, it is nevertheless part of the poem's achievement that this failure of energy and nerve—if that is what it is—finds in *In Memoriam* its proper cadence.

Doubtless Tennyson himself was not content with achievement of that kind. His own description of *In Memoriam* as "the way of the soul" (he compared it to Dante's *Commedia*) would seem to claim a more positive accomplishment, a more sustaining theme. And yet the poem betrays no little vacillation on the question of its own intent and value; the old uncertainty as to whether a poet's first duty is to explore his private sensibility or to enlighten public sentiment is strongly evident. The poem repeatedly disparages itself; Tennyson insists (XLVIII) that his "brief lays" close no grave doubts, propose no answers. Such songs, he feels, are vain (LXXVI); but, worse still, their preoccupation with personal sorrow is "half a sin" (V).

On the one hand, they cannot do justice to his deepest feelings; and, on the other, they may be a kind of self-indulgence. In Canto XXI the poet imagines various reactions to his songs of mourning: one may think him weak and his sorrowing an encouragement to weakness; another may dismiss his songs as a display of emotion to gain pity and praise; a third may ask, "Is this an hour/For private sorrow's barren song?" The poet defends his grief as a kind of natural reflex, but we see a continuation of the inward debate between Tennyson's two voices. The debate persists as Tennyson asks, "What hope is here for modern rhyme?" (LXXVII); and he bitterly supposes that his "mortal lullabies of pain . . ." are doomed to desecration as the scraps of paper that "serve to curl a maiden's locks." The reply is merely a stubborn loyalty to sorrow: "To breathe my loss is more than fame,/To utter love more sweet than praise."

In Canto LXIX the poet dreams that he wears his grief like a crown of thorns. The symbol meets with public scorn—"They call'd me fool, they call'd me child"—but "an angel of the night" seems to touch the crown into leaf and to approve the poet's dedicated mourning. However, the emphasis shifts. The Prologue—one of the last pieces to be added to the series—rather than an introduction, stands as almost a conventional palinode: "Forgive these wild and wandering cries,/Confusions of a wasted youth." Uppermost here is a sense that an outpouring of personal sorrow and spiritual travail is something a poet must answer for.

Tennyson's mixed allegiance—his need to honor his grief and his duty to overcome it—is in itself, then, an important strain in the poem. It also accounts, probably, for the alternation between those sections that simply record the fluctuations in the poet's feelings, the various forms his bereavement takes, and those in which a homiletic quality gains supremacy. Typical of this latter tone is Canto LIII with its concluding exhortation:

Hold thou the good, define it well;
For fear divine Philosophy
Should push beyond her mark, and be
Procuress to the Lords of Hell.

And yet the very next section ends with one of Tennyson's most penetrating moments of self-awareness:

So runs my dream; but what am I?
An infant crying in the night;
An infant crying for the light,
And with no language but a cry.
(LIV)

The sage's confident guise is abandoned—Tennyson yields to the helplessness and terror which his sense of loss has left him. The real life of *In Memoriam,* we feel, is exemplified more by the second passage than by the first; and this judgment points to one cause of the poem's considerable unevenness.

This is not to say that ideas and convictions are of no account in the poem. Indeed, it is common to read *In Memoriam* either as a theodicy or as a gloss on nineteenth-century science, reflecting discoveries in geology and anticipating Darwinian theory. However, as religious profession, it is both inconsistent and unsophisticated; and the conclusions it draws from science are often not very scientific. Tennyson was occupied with his elegies during a period when he had embarked upon a rather ambitious and varied program of self-education, and it is only natural that his reading—Sir Charles Lyell, Sir William Herschel, Robert Chambers, Carlyle—found its way into these most personal poems. Yet the informing spirit of *In Memoriam* did not come from Tennyson's library, nor even from his intellectual *milieu.* Tennyson used current notions and concerns in his poem as illustrations; he did not create the poem as an illustration of them. Hence one does not find, nor is one entitled to expect, the intellectual coherence of the philosophical poem—of Lucretius's *De rerum natura,* of Spenser's *Four Hymns,* of Sir John Davies's *Orchestra,* or Pope's *Essay on Man.* Moreover, it also lacks the visionary scope that Tennyson's own phrase "the way of the soul" *might* lead one to expect. *In Memoriam* is obviously not a systematic exposition; it is, as T. S. Eliot rightly judged, a kind of emotional diary[31] or series of poetic meditations that circle around the crucial experience of the poet's life.

Hallam's loss was crucial, as *In Memoriam* makes clear, because it crystallized into "one pure image of regret" (CII) that poignant sense of transience and all those various longings and deprivations that constitute Tennyson's passion of the past. Such was the nature of this loss, and such the range of Tennyson's response to it, that the many guises in which he was wont to express this passion —guises of abandonment, disinheritance, and guilty exile—are encompassed by it. The poem reaches out in many directions in its concern with human mortality, but what moves Tennyson most deeply is the mere fact of separation. Hallam is, beyond all else, "My Arthur, whom I shall not see" (IX, echoed in XVII). The poem's pity is self-pity; for, whatever may be surmised about the dead, to live is to endure the death-in-life of bereavement. Amid Tennyson's myriad doubts concerning the meaning of death, his awareness of separation from his friend stands out as a simple and incontrovertible certainty: "My paths are in the fields I know,/And thine in undiscover'd lands." [32] (XL).

As do other great elegies, *In Memoriam* attempts to develop its commemoration of a particular death into a contemplation of our common fate. Tennyson imagines Hallam's remains borne home within the ship and frames his version of the eternal question: "Is this the end? Is this the end?" (XII). Nevertheless, the rather general assumption that the poem's chief concern is the reconciliation to death[33] is somewhat misleading. The poet's "feud with Death" results from his blighted human friendship:

For this alone on Death I wreak
　The wrath that garners in my heart:
　He put our lives so far apart
We cannot hear each other speak.
(LXXXII)

Certainly *In Memoriam* is not merely concerned abstractly with the question of immortality; what death must mean to the living —not what it might mean for the dead—is the primary subject. In Canto XL, for example, Tennyson can imagine his dead friend as like a bride who has merely left one home for another; but, when he thinks not of the dead but of the living, the analogy collapses:

Ay me, the difference I discern!
　How often shall her old fireside
　Be cheer'd with tidings of the bride,
How often she herself return.

Again, in the lyric that follows, Tennyson asserts that "my nature rarely yields/To that vague fear implied in death"; a more chilling thought is "that I shall be thy mate no more" (XLI).

"This," as Tennyson says in another poem, "is the curse of time";[34] time is "a maniac scattering dust" (L), effecting a senseless severance from all we love in the past. The sense of temporal dislocation we have marked in Tennyson's other lyrics is frequently acute in *In Memoriam.* It is masterfully evoked in Canto VII ("Dark house"), where the poet's alienation from present existence is likened to the feeling of guilt, and where everything has the hideous strangeness of a nightmare:

And like a guilty thing I creep
　At earliest morning to the door.

He is not here; but far away
The noise of life begins again,
And ghastly thro' the drizzling rain
On the bald street breaks the blank day.

Elsewhere life is depicted as a desolate and lonely path, with "prospect and horizon gone" (XXXVIII), "changed from where it ran/Thro' lands where not a leaf was dumb, . . . and all was good that Time could bring" (XXIII). In the abandonment of the present, the future can only seem a "secular abyss" (LXXVI).

When expressing such feelings, Tennyson's imagistic powers are often at their height. Canto II makes of an "Old yew, which graspest at the stones/That name the underlying dead" a symbol of rich and apt suggestiveness. That tree stands in the midst of nature's endless regeneration, starkly at odds with the world of process, its roots clasping the dead whose graves are there:

O, not for thee the glow, the bloom,
Who changest not in any gale,
Nor branding summer suns avail
To touch thy thousand years of gloom.

With fine economy the poem contrasts the eternal cycle of life with the yew's changeless gloom. In the tree, the poet beholds his own ideal fidelity to the dead past amid the living flux, and so identifies himself with the "sullen tree," which represents, like Tennyson's "Tithonus," "Immortal age beside immortal youth": "I seem to fail from out my blood/And grow incorporate into thee."

This sense of estrangement from the living present brings with it, as in so many of Tennyson's poems, a concern with memory. Indeed, the elegy is not only *in memoriam,* it is essentially *de memoria;* nothing in the poem comes closer to being a unifying theme. Canto I, which is more truly than the Prologue the real beginning, renounces the progressive assumption "that men may rise on stepping-stones/Of their dead selves to higher things"; for no prospect of future fulfillment can compensate for present sorrow or substitute for past joy. Moreover, only by clinging to that remembrance which is grief can love—the ultimate reality, the essential value—be preserved: "Let Love clasp Grief lest both be drown'd."

Hence, we have the paradox of Sorrow's "cruel fellowship" (III); it is the implicit irony of *In Memoriam* that to attain consolation would be to confront a still deeper anguish. While the poet can "weep a loss for ever new" (XIII), while the memory of his friend remains fresh enough to be painful, love must be real, must indeed transcend the material dimensions of time and space. "I long to prove," writes Tennyson in Canto XXVI, "No lapse of moons can canker Love"; and to that end sorrow must be claimed as "No casual mistress, but a wife" (LIX).

I grieve, therefore love is might be a fair statement of the proposition that in one way or another underlies much of *In Memoriam.* It is a crucial affirmation; for since his love for Hallam, "which masters Time" (LXXXV), is an earthly counterpart of that "immortal Love" which Tennyson invokes in the Prologue, such love testifies in a world of sense to the reality of spirit. If "human love and truth" are not "As dying Nature's earth and lime" (CXVIII), there are grounds for rejecting the naturalistic premise, to which the poem makes many a troubled reference, that men are "only cunning casts in clay" (CXX) and for affirming love as "Creation's final law" (LVI). This affirmation is, of course, what lies behind the famous sentiment:

I hold it true, whate'er befall;
I feel it, when I sorrow most;
'T is better to have loved and lost
Than never to have loved at all.
(XXVII)

Fidelity, through memory, to human love confirms human spirituality.

Thus, Tennyson from the emptiness of the present casts his mind back upon his friend, "To whom a thousand memories call" (CXI); and, in so doing, he not only illustrates the proposition *I grieve, therefore love is,* but also moves toward a more fundamental assertion: *I remember, therefore I am.* For memory is sought not only in substantiation of love but also as a means of being. His friend lives *in* memory, but the poet himself would establish his own existence *through* memory. This conception is the same as that explicitly set forth in a passage in *The Lover's Tale* (ll. 112–19), where the narrator, Julian, says that his life is neither "in the present time,/Nor in the present place." "In that I *have* lived," he continues, "do I live,/And cannot die, and am, in having been."

Similarly, Canto XLV of *In Memoriam* suggests, through its interestingly modern notions about the development of self-consciousness in the child, that memory is essential to human identity. The poem concludes that a growing isolation is the necessary price of this developing self-awareness; but, if full existence implies inevitable isolation within the self, isolation from one's past self is oblivion. In those sections that treat the Tennyson family's removal from Somersby (C–CIV), this weakening of the poet's bonds with the past seems like a second death of his friend and the attenuation of his own existence.

As we might expect, this relationship between memory and the fullest sense of being plays a significant part in Tennyson's speculations on the hereafter. Instinctively, and, in view of the conceptions just noted, not illogically, he imagines eternal bliss as the recovery of the past:

> So then were nothing lost to man;
> So that still garden of the souls
> In many a figured leaf enrolls
> The total world since life began.
> (XLIII)

In death "we close with all we loved/And all we flow from" (CXXXI); the soul's attainment of essential knowledge in that state of complete being which constitutes the "spiritual prime" (XLIII) beyond the grave is identified as a vista of "The eternal landscape of the past" (XLVI).

Yet to the earth-bound poet memory remains an imperfect and painful recourse. And the shape Tennyson finally gave his collection of elegies stresses an increasing desire to escape from inert nostalgia and somehow still be faithful to his lost friend. In the later sections of the poem Hallam, accordingly, becomes less a shadow of the past and more of a beacon from the future. For he is, finally, both a type of human earthly perfection and, we might almost say, Tennyson's Beatrice—a link between this world and the next. The quality of the poet's attachment to Hallam modulates correspondingly. Canto CX speaks of a "vague desire/That spurs an imitative will"—no doubt a more sustaining but, it must be admitted, a less poignant love than the longings of the child crying in the night that characterize earlier sections.

From this altered vision of what the dead friend and Tennyson's relation to him represent emerges such consolation as *In Memoriam* contains. A crucial figuring forth of that revised conception is found in Canto CXXI, one of the last written and most accomplished of all the elegies:

> Sad Hesper o'er the buried sun
> And ready, thou, to die with him,
> Thou watchest all things ever dim
> And dimmer, and a glory done.
>
> The team is loosen'd from the wain,
> The boat is drawn upon the shore;
> Thou listenest to the closing door,
> And life is darken'd in the brain.
>
> Bright Phosphor, fresher for the night,
> By thee the world's great work is heard
> Beginning, and the wakeful bird;
> Behind thee comes the greater light.
>
> The market boat is on the stream,
> And voices hail it from the brink;
> Thou hear'st the village hammer clink,
> And see'st the moving of the team.
>
> Sweet Hesper-Phosphor, double name
> For what is one, the first, the last,
> Thou, like my present and my past,
> Thy place is changed; thou art the same.

The evening star, presiding over the dying day, and the morning star, herald of bright beginning, are but different manifestations of the planet Venus. In this unity is symbolized the constancy of the poet's love as grief gives way to hope. More broadly, it is the miracle of regeneration, of continuity, that the poem affirms. Past and present are here not severed by the curse of time but bound in identity; and, just as Hesperus and Phosphor are both Love's star, so even life and death, in the light of that immortal Love Tennyson invokes in his Prologue—encompassing as it does the alpha and omega—can be but parts of a single whole.

Thus *In Memoriam*'s pervading emphasis on alienation and discontinuity is succeeded at length by a celebration of natural and human process. At Canto CVI ("Ring out, wild bells") there is a turn toward the "to be" and the epithalamium-like Epilogue ends the poem in an emphatic tribute to generation. Being less a matter of rational argument than of emotional testimony, this transformation of the poet's outlook is especially marked at the level of image and metaphor. In place of the old yew, that "sullen tree" untouched by the seasons' return, now stands something more like Yeats's great rooted blossomer (or Carlyle's Igdrasil): "For all we thought and loved and did,/And hoped, and suffer'd is but seed/Of what in them is flower and fruit" (Epilogue, ll. 134–36). Thus the secular hope and the divine come together, not because they are identical but because both are nourished by the same affirmations: the whole manifesting itself from the part, limitation seen as only the negative guise of potentiality, the imperfect not denying but indeed declaring the possibility of perfection: "I see in part/That all, as in some piece of art,/Is toil coöperant to an end" (CXXVIII).

Of Tennyson's conception of what lies beyond death, as revealed in *In Memoriam,* T. S. Eliot has observed that "his concern is for the loss of man rather than for the gain of God."[35] Certainly the poem does not evoke future bliss with anything like the intensity with which it expresses the loss of past joy. However, it is not merely that Tennyson's grief is more deeply felt than his faith—inevitable to the modern reader as such a conclusion might be. What too often overtakes Tennyson's imagination when it confronts the "hereafter" is a naive and homely literalness. We are not moved, but embarrassed, when, speaking of Hallam in Canto LXXV, he writes that "somewhere, out of human view,/Whate'er thy hands are set to do/Is wrought with tumult of acclaim." Is this picture of Hallam winning angelic applause by some vague feat of dexterity any more disconcerting, it might be asked, than that of the saints above drying the eyes of Milton's drowned Lycidas?

The answer must be an emphatic "yes," and the reason is mainly that, whereas Milton's image depends upon its link to the Book of Revelation and hence demands a response to traditional associations, Tennyson's leaves the reader with only the choice between gauche literalism and pointless, improvised analogy. We see in this the misfortune of religious poetry that was written in a period of enfeebled tradition, but the failing is also an individual one. *In Memoriam* would be far more impressive as a whole were it not for Tennyson's irksome affinity for the bathetic, the coy, and the hackneyed in choosing similes by which to express various aspects of the spiritual relation between the mortal poet and his immortal friend.[36]

But—despite such lapses, and they are numerous—*In Memoriam* remains one of the grand achievements of English poetry. Some of its lyrics have a remarkable perfection, and hardly one of them is untouched by the resonance that results when emotion and expression are finely attuned. This quality is well illustrated by a contrast Eleanor Mattes has pointed to between a passage from *In Memoriam* and its apparent source in Lyell's *Principles of Geology*. Lyell wrote that "millions of our race are now supported by lands situated where deep seas prevailed in earlier ages"; Tennyson paraphrases this statement in the lines: "There where the long street roars hath been/The stillness of the central sea."[37] (CXXIII). There is no falsification; the poet is as unmelodramatic and nearly as precise as the geologist, but his attention to the perfectly natural contrast between the noisy thoroughfare and the silent face of the deep informs not only the understanding but the emotions. Lyell conveys only the fact; Tennyson has evoked the awe that, for some minds at least, must be part of that fact's meaning.

Such examples remind us not to view Tennyson's *In Memoriam* as only a relic of nineteenth-century intellectual history. The concerns of the man and his hour become, again and again, apt terms in which are framed the eternal confrontation by human consciousness of its perpetually astounding circumstances.

V *Occasional Verse: Commemorative, Dedicatory, Epistolary, and Satiric*

This chapter on Tennyson as a lyric poet concludes with a glance at several varieties of verse that can all be classified as "occasional"—a designation that applies, at least loosely, to the origin and manner of a considerable number of poems. *In Memoriam* is itself the greatest of Tennyson's occasional poems, though the term hardly characterizes a work that comprehends so much of its author's experience and sensibility.

A sizable segment of Tennyson's occasional verse may be described as "commemorative," poems that honor public figures or personal friends at their deaths or that celebrate national exploits or ceremonies of state. Of course many of these were laureate performances. Tennyson dutifully welcomed in verse foreign royalty preparing to marry English and English royalty that had married foreign; his verses graced the openings of international and colonial exhibitions; and he recorded appropriate sentiments on Victoria's jubilee.

If we exempt *In Memoriam,* as having vaster and more complex intentions, the most important among these commemorative works is certainly the "Ode on the Death of the Duke of Wellington," published on the day of Wellington's funeral in 1852 but much revised when reprinted the following year. A stately and sonorous poem, an onomatopoeic *tour de force,* it contains among its funereal effects those of muffled drums, choric song, tolling bells, and a cannon salute. But it is more than a formal tribute to a great, if personally unendearing, national hero; what Tennyson makes of the occasion reveals itself in a comparison, along certain lines, between the Wellington ode and *In Memoriam.* Like the elegy on Hallam, the ode on the victor of Waterloo fixes upon the personage it memorializes as a type of human excellence and a testimony, in the face of natural vicissitude, to the worth and promise of the human soul:

> Tho' world on world in myriad myriads roll
> Round us, each with different powers,
> And other forms of life than ours,
> What know we greater than the soul?
> (ll. 262–65)

This passage, with a minor adjustment in the meter, could pass as a stanza out of *In Memoriam,* so close is it to that poem's prevailing tone and sentiment. In Wellington, as in Hallam, Tennyson mourns the passing of a figure whose perfections no successor can rival; the Duke is "the last great Englishman." But, as he attempted to do in his elegy, Tennyson finds in this man's preeminence greater cause for gratitude and hope than for dispiriting nostalgia. The hero is an example of human possibility and also of divine providence; in a spirit reminiscent of Carlyle's hero worship, Tennyson affirms that "On God and Godlike men we build our trust" (1. 266).

Naturally there are differences in the two poems that are at least as instructive as the similarities. *In Memoriam* is permeated by private doubt; the Wellington ode, though never indecorous, exudes public confidence. Hallam, after all, left his friend desolate and uncertain even that such virtues find a reward; but Wellington died with his fame secure and his country powerful. It must even be admitted that, in a limited sense, the ode is the more successful poem; for Wellington serves more adequately the symbolic function assigned him than does Hallam. The young intellectual may be more appealing than the statesman-warrior—and of course Tennyson's own feelings for the former were infinitely stronger; but, for all that, Wellington the public figure is a more meaningful embodiment of the triumphant life than is the poet's friend. All dead friends are paragons; and, because all are, we suspect none may be. But, because the hero's deeds and supposed virtues have become public possessions, they are, in terms of their poetic viability, undeniably his own.

A second category of occasional verse comprises poems addressed to individuals. Many of these are dedicatory; and, though dedications seldom add to the distinction of the larger work or volume which they accompany, Tennyson's are marked at least by an appropriate adaptation of tone to the rhetorical situation and by sufficient grace to rise above the perfunctory without becoming fulsome. The verse inscription to Edward FitzGerald that introduces "Tiresias" glows with the easy bantering and warm regard of an old friendship; that to Professor Jebb which accompanies "Demeter and Persephone" is as crisp and deft as a classicist could wish. The *Idylls of the King* is prefaced by a "Dedication" to the memory of the Prince Consort and concludes with an epilogue "To the Queen"; and together they bestow something of epic dignity upon Victoria's grief for her beloved Albert and even upon the cause of empire, while at the same time tactfully claiming for this "new-old" tale the Prince's admiration and sketching for the Queen what Tennyson referred to as its "parabolic drift." In dedicating the *Demeter* volume to Lord Dufferin, he takes occasion to eulogize his own son, Lionel; for Lord Dufferin by his kindness to the stricken son was a most fitting audience for a bereaved father's feelings.

Such a piece as the charming "To Mary Boyle" shows Tennyson's often overlooked skill with the verse epistle. More characteristic, perhaps, is the formal solemnity of his poems "To J.S." [James Spedding], "To E. [Edward] L. [Lear], on his Travels in Greece," and, if poems to dead masters may be included, "To Virgil." But these works have not the freshness Tennyson can muster when he affects the epistolary manner, as he does in the poem to FitzGerald mentioned above, in "To Ulysses" (W. G. Palgrave), "The Daisy" (to Mrs. Tennyson), and especially in "To the Rev. F. D. Maurice." The letter to Maurice strikes so genial and humane a note in its offer of refuge and good company to that hard-pressed spokesman for religious liberalism that one is sent back to Ben Jonson to find anything as choice in the same vein:

> Should all our churchmen foam in spite
> At you, so careful of the right,
>   Yet one lay-hearth would give you welcome—
>   Take it and come—to the Isle of Wight.

This chapter must stop far short of an exhaustive catalogue and survey of all the lyric sub-species at which Tennyson tried his hand. But one other classification of occasional poems should be mentioned: those of a satirical cast. For satire Tennyson had a persistent though by no means commanding flair. It appears in *The Princess,* in some of the misbegotten "lady" poems, in the "Northern Farmer" pieces, in "Sea Dreams," and even—shading into invective—in the two Locksley Hall poems and in *Maud.* In those works where some form of satire is the chief substance, Tennyson tends to assume one of two contrary but equally unbecoming manners: a stilted archness or a splenetic snarl. The former is most common in Tennyson's earliest verse, in such mechanic exercises as "Lines: to the Picture of a Young Lady of Fashion" (*UEP*) and the "Three Sonnets to a Coquette." There is nothing to these thrusts at female vanity but the shallowest literary pretense; when the young Tennyson swung his sights to the plight of poetry or the folly of poets, as in "What Thor Said" and "Amphion," the result is still thin but also more genuinely amusing.

When, on the other hand, Tennyson is stung into satire by actual criticism of himself, the counterblast has more the quality of a sudden reflex than of the cunning stroke of a really gifted satirist. In such salvos as "To Christopher North" and "The New Timon and the Poets" (in answer to Bulwer-Lytton) we see something of the black-blooded Tennyson who is reported to have received the mild strictures of Benjamin Jowett upon some of his verses by savagely denouncing the sherry which the Master of Balliol had served him. "The New Timon," as a strong antidote to the "Schoolmiss Alfred" style of some early Tennyson, is not without value, but, even when indignation is pungently expressed, it is no substitute for wit. Tennyson, however, was more inclined to repent of satire than to cultivate it. The pious wife in "Sea Dreams" declares that "he had never kindly heart,/Nor ever cared to better his own kind,/Who first wrote satire, with no pity in it." A large portion of Tennyson's public, as well as a strong element in his own nature, held with that sentiment.

CHAPTER 3

The Narrative Poet

SINCE T. S. Eliot advanced the view, it has been generally accepted that "for narrative Tennyson had no gift at all."[1] His talents lay—it is common, following Eliot, to assert—not in recounting the flow of events but in rendering the more or less arrested scene or incident—in the composition, that is to say, of idylls.[2] The larger works are described as being either idylls that are too long (*The Princess, Enoch Arden*) or, in the obvious case of the *Idylls of the King,* a collection of such poems, which, moreover, tend individually to consist of a succession of picturesque moments. There is no disputing the essential truth of this view, except that it implies a rather too narrow conception of "narrative" as straightforward tale-telling—a conception hardly applicable to Homer, to say nothing of most modern novelists.

Tennyson was not greatly inventive when it came to narrative subjects; typically, he drew upon anecdotes told him by friends (*Enoch Arden*), the current prose tales be read ("The Miller's Daughter," "Dora"), and traditional legends ("Godiva," "The Voyage of Maeldune," *Idylls of the King*). When he does originate, and indeed when he borrows, he shows a distressingly consistent affinity for situations that are hackneyed and sentimental. And, as Eliot and others have noted, his interest is less in actions than in pictures and moods.

An extreme example, but nonetheless indicative of Tennyson's common practice, is "The Day-Dream," a Tennysonian version of "The Sleeping Beauty." It is a series of poems, each focused upon one stage of the familiar story; Tennyson does not so much *retell* the fairy tale as *illustrate* it. As an instance of how Tennyson responds to narrative material, "The Day-Dream" is also instructive in other respects. It grew from a single lyric: a picture-like description of the Sleeping Beauty. Later Tennyson added the other sections to represent the story as a sequence of "stills"; at the same time—and this is characteristic—he "framed" the legend by giving it a modern context and by making it the occasion for reflections that, although they rather belittle the tale itself, register a certain unwillingness to have it taken merely for what it is. Thus are anticipated in this early poem some crucial shaping tendencies of the author of *The Princess, Maud,*[3] and *Idylls of the King.*

For, even though we understand what Eliot meant in declaring that Tennyson's poems "are never really narrative," [4] it was nonetheless a mode in which, after his own fashion, Tennyson expended a major portion of his energies, and one to which, after all, a number of his most important works in some sense belong. Nor can we escape the conclusion that Tennyson regarded one of the poet's inherent capacities to be that of storyteller. When the question of a suitable subject for a great work came up, as it often did, commanding not only the Laureate's own thoughts but those of his wife, his friends, and the reviewers as well, it was usually narrative material that was considered. H. M. McLuhan finds the prototype of Tennyson's art in the "idyllic or picture method" of Theocritus.[5] Other, more homely traditions which lie behind his narrative productions are those of the ballad and of the dream allegory. These forms, in fact, are like two tributaries feeding his narrative poetry through its course of development.

A strong ballad influence can be traced in Tennyson's work from such early poems as "Mariana" and "The Lady of Shalott" to his final volume where, for "The Bandit's Death," he borrowed a story from Walter Scott. Simple incidents baldly sketched, or only implied, and a stylized manner, in which the song-like voice of the poet imposes itself deliberately between the subject and the audience, are perhaps the instinctive recourse of a lyric talent when essaying narrative. That essential aspects of Tennyson's narrative art derive from the ballad-maker's stock in trade is suggested by an examination of a pair of early works that come about as close to the conventional literary ballad as anything Tennyson attempted.

"The Ballad of Oriana" (1830) tells of the remorse of a champion whose arrow, intended for his foeman, flew wide of its mark and slew his beloved. "The Sisters" (1832), a much superior effort, presents the story of a damsel, driven no less by jealousy and perverse desire than by outraged honor, who wins her sister's seducer with her charms and then stabs him in bed. Here, unquestionably, is the proper stuff for ballad treatment; but it is equally clear that here, at least in embryo, are important Tennysonian motifs. The lover whose guilty deed or other mark of unworthiness puts his loved one beyond reach, family pride trampled upon, the furious love-hatred of a woman scorned subduing masculinity—Tennyson would ring the changes on these themes throughout his career. And, in noticing such resemblances, we are reminded how other situations Tennyson treats poetically have about them this same ballad-like simplicity, a kind of naive dependence on obvious and strong effects.

When the guise of storyteller did not call forth in Tennyson something of the balladeer's ways and means, it alternately cast him back upon allegory or the dream vision, or upon that convention which combines the two. Among Tennyson's earliest extant narrative works are the vision poems "Armageddon" and "Timbuctoo," the latter a drastic revision and expansion of the first, "The Coach of Death," and the more strictly allegorical "Sense and Conscience." "Recollections of the Arabian Nights" (1830), and "A Dream of Fair Women" (1832) are simply sensuous evocations of Tennyson's literary memories, but "The Palace of Art" (1832) and "The Vision of Sin" (1842) show Tennyson's attraction to the dream allegory tradition. It may be added that the monologue "Oenone," another product of Tennyson's formative years, has as its center an allegorical account of the judgment of Paris.

So strong a penchant for allegory as is evident in the early poetry made it natural that Tennyson's major narrative work, the *Idylls of the King,* should contain what he himself described as a "parabolic drift." Yet the first *Idylls* were not conceived as allegory. The "Morte d'Arthur," though expressive of the passing of the old order, is scarcely allegorical, nor are the four *Idylls* published in 1859. These works bear, rather, the marks of the other narrative manner favored by Tennyson: that of the ballad, or the ballad-like idyll—a development to be discussed shortly.

In their completed form, then, the *Idylls of the King* reveal a confluence of both the balladesque and allegorical impulses; and to each of these two lines can be attached dominant qualities of Tennyson's narrative poetry as a whole: sentimentalism and melodrama, on the one hand; didacticism, on the other. That is to say, these qualities tend to result when Tennyson adapts aspects of his rather modest prototypes to more pretentious artistic purposes. A ballad-like situation, unchecked by the terseness and understatement inherent in the form, is subject to inflations of either a sentimental or melodramatic sort. The moral point we expect in simple allegory can become irksome moralizing in a work whose rich orchestration seems to promise something less obvious and more profound.

I *English Idyls,*[6] Enoch Arden

In the *Collected Edition* of 1884 Tennyson designated a large group of his works as "English Idyls." It is a loose classification; what such poems have in common is a certain aura of idealized simplicity and subdued nostalgia, along with a modesty of scope that confines itself to the brief depiction of character or situation in a setting one would call Arcadian if it were not so very English. They form, on the whole, a rather uninteresting group of poems; but they played an important part in establishing Tennyson's contemporary reputation; and they also constitute a range of poetic manner and effect of which his more distinguished work is in many ways only a finer realization.

The most notable outcropping of this type of poem occurs in the volumes of 1842; however, earlier poems like "The May Queen" and "The Miller's Daughter" are in the same vein, and Tennyson continued to write English idyls all his life. They mark, as is often said, a turning from the intenser introspections and more flamboyant attitudes of Tennyson's youth toward a more public manner calculated to stir gently the feelings rather than to startle the sensibility. Though recognizable as a type, these domestic idyls are—even if extreme in no other sense—extremely miscellaneous, both as a group and in many cases as single poems. Tennyson often employs first-person narrative, but third person is also common. "Walking to the Mail" and "The Talking Oak," however, are composed of dialogue. Some idyls, "Dora" is a prime example, consist of the straightforward telling of a tale. Others, like "Walking to the Mail" are made up of disconnected bits of gossip. Some glance at political topics; one, "Aylmer's Field," reaches its climax in a piece of scourging pulpit oratory. It is a favorite practice of Tennyson to shore up a rather slender bit of narrative by interjecting a song or lyric passage.

As an example of the kind of mixed bag such diverse materials produced, we have "The Brook" (1855). In that poem the narrator, Lawrence Aylmer, muses upon his dead brother. He then recalls a talkative neighbor, Philip, whose farm lies near, and Philip's fair daughter Katie. Lawrence recounts the good turn he once did Katie by serving as an audience for her father while she and her lover, James, seize the occasion to patch a quarrel. Interspersed are snatches of the song of the brook—rhymes made by the dead brother Edmund, who had been a promising poet. Finally, the narrative voice shifts to third person; and the poem concludes with Lawrence's encountering the daughter of that same Katie Willows, returned from Australia, and his being invited inside to renew his old acquaintance with the mother.

Yet the poem itself seems somewhat less of a hotchpotch than this summary suggests, and the wonder is that it hangs together at all. Such unity as it has is achieved through a pervasive tone—in this case, a wistful sense of what Tennyson spoke of as "the abiding in the transient," rather tritely epitomized in the brook's refrain: "For men may come and men may go,/But I go on for ever." Similarly, Tennyson attempts in the other idyls, with varying success of course, to let tone or atmosphere supply a unity or wholeness the subject may lack.

To this end he employs, from poem to poem, a range of styles: the smothering ornamentation of "The Gardener's Daughter," the minutely exact vividness of "The Miller's Daughter," Wordsworthian ruggedness in the homely "Dora," Wordsworthian playfulness in the jingling near-doggerel of "The Talking Oak." Style, however, especially when it amounts only to mannerism, cannot always answer as a unifying element. Miscellaneousness is so much a quality of the English idyls that they make us feel we are confronting poems uncontrolled by any inner logic—swatches of "poetic stuff" rather than shaped works. Then we may be moved to ask, like the narrator in "Edwin Morris," "Were not his words delicious, I a beast/To take them as I did?" But when the words are not "delicious"—when even Tennyson's powers of language are unengaged—only banality remains:

'And when does this come by?'
'The mail? At one o'clock.'
'What is it now?'
'A quarter to.'

T. S. Eliot was to turn such aridity to striking account in *The Waste Land;* but his scene is rats' alley, not an English country road.

One way Tennyson sometimes gives the idyl greater formal integrity is to grant more distinctiveness and more dramatic substance to the narrative voice and so move toward the dramatic monologue; but poems of this kind are considered in the chapter on dramatic verse. Another way is to focus upon the narrative element itself, and accordingly some idyls ("Lady Clare," "The Lord of Burleigh") preserve a ballad-like flavor. These examples are perhaps not distinguished poems, but they exhibit a workmanlike tidiness that comes from clarity of conception and from the controlling influence of a more or less defined effect. Incidentally, they form a pair of antithetical treatments of the theme of "unequal" marriage, each turning upon the revelation of true identity that would become a recurrent motif in *Idylls of the King.*

One commentator characterizes Tennyson's idyls as "contrived exercises in objectivity, each in its way an escape from personal commitment and the burden of the self." [7] Although this fairly distinguishes them from the spontaneous overflow of powerful feelings, it should not mislead us to the conclusion that these poems somehow lie wholly beyond the world of their author's private concerns. Reading the idyls from the 1842 volumes, one would not, for instance, find it strange to learn that the period most productive of this kind of poem was also one during which Tennyson formed at least two romantic attachments, experienced divers obstacles to happy marriage, and both deplored his single state and burrowed deeper into bachelorhood.

It seems certain that "The Gardener's Daughter" and "Edwin Morris" reflect rather directly two phases of Tennyson's acquaintance with Rosa Baring;[8] and, if the love song to Ellen Aubrey in "Audley Court" is not precisely an expression of the poet's love for Emily Sellwood, in the characters of the narrator and his friend Francis Hale might be seen Tennyson's own contrasting attitudes toward women. Each seems an alternative strategy for keeping a decisive involvement at arm's length—one, by evoking an idealized conception; the other, by affecting an air of carefree cynicism. Frequently in these idyls Tennyson shows a preference for contemplating feminine charms from a safe vantage point, in the "painterly" fashion of "The Gardener's Daughter" or, as in "Audley Court" and "The Day-Dream," praising the lady while she sleeps.

A different manifestation of his morbid shyness appears in "Godiva." The truest note in that narrative, certainly its emotional center, is the passage describing Godiva's cringing fear in exposing her nakedness: "the blind walls/Were full of chinks and holes; and overhead/Fantastic gables, crowding, stared." Her timidity is much more vividly imagined than her human sympathy that overcomes it; for it is as if Tennyson, who had writhed beneath the ruthless scrutiny of the reviews, imparted some of his own detestation of the public eye. It would be too much to see in "Godiva" a direct analogue for the poet's own kind of gallantry and risk, but we do know that Tennyson considered both carping criticism and prying biography "a sense misused" and would have wished upon all literary Peeping Toms no better fate than befell the original:

> For now the Poet cannot die,
> Nor leave his music as of old,
> But round him ere he scarce be cold
> Begins the scandal and the cry:
>
> 'Proclaim the faults he would not show;
> Break lock and seal, betray the trust;
> Keep nothing sacred, 't is but just
> The many-headed beast should know.'
> ("To ———,: After Reading a
> Life and Letters")

Enoch Arden is the culmination—not chronologically but artistically—of much that is involved in Tennyson's exploitation of the idyllic. The touching story of the fisherman lost on a voyage from which he belatedly returns to find his wife married to a friend, and who thereupon stifles his longing and chooses to remain undisclosed in order to preserve the happiness of those he loves, the picturesque scenes in the little fishing village, out nutting in the woods, on Enoch's desert isle, around Annie's cheerful hearth; and the delineation of the simple but heroic virtues of constancy, generosity, and devoted self-sacrifice are wrought to their uttermost. It is, withal, a poem almost wholly beyond the pale of modern appreciation.

Nonetheless (perhaps all the more), *Enoch Arden* has a particular importance in any full and just encounter with Tennyson's work. There is a perverse charity in the alternative explanations that Tennyson in *Enoch Arden* was yielding to the deplorable taste of the mid-Victorian era or that the poem is simply a failure, that Tennyson floundered in confusion between a realistic and a heightened poetic treatment of his subject. Neither of these views quite faces up to the poem. In *Enoch Arden*, Tennyson's own instincts are in full command; and what we disapprove of is not his failure but his success. Behind Tennyson's own slightly fatuous description of the poem as "a very perfect thing" lies a certain truth; no doubt Tennyson realized from Woolner's tale, the source of the poem, every potential he imagined it to have. Nor is this supposition intended merely as mock praise. For Tennyson the story of Enoch is a gamut of sentimental effects; but, even while wincing at the sentimentalism, we must note the sureness of touch with which the effects are achieved. The question was recently posed in a journal devoted to Victorian culture whether "ugliness" itself cannot be sometimes successful. It is no more paradoxical to ask whether sentimentality cannot be masterfully executed. *Enoch Arden* is a definitive expression of *Schmalz*—a most genuine piece of British Biedermeier[9]—and deserves at the very least the respect that authenticity of any kind commands.

At every point Tennyson finds the way to draw a maximum of tender feeling, of poignant atmosphere, from his material. The alternation of styles from the simple to the ornate, from the realistic to the elevated, that critics have condemned, is explained, if not justified, by the fact that neither verisimilitude nor decorum but a kind of emotional pragmatism is the governing principle. Whether Enoch's words are those of a sage or a rude fisherman depends upon whether the effect to be wrung from a particular dramatic context is that of a moving nobility or a touching downrightness.

The carefully managed opening illustrates Tennyson's artfulness in enveloping his narrative with an aura in which small things seem as precious as great and all is tinged with gentle pathos. The poem's initial lines frame an intimate scene of the story's three principals, playing together in the sand as children "a hundred years ago," against a background of the village, the countryside, and the vast stretch of rugged and timeless shoreline. Here Annie Lee, Philip Ray, and Enoch Arden

built their castles of dissolving sand
To watch them overflow'd, or following up
And flying the white breaker, daily left
The little footprint daily wash'd away.

The scene evokes a vision of human life as a tiny but vivid moment in the eternal ebb and flow; and, though such a vision is not precisely integral to the story itself, it creates an ambience calculated to enhance the dignity of the fable. There follows a piece of sentimental foreshadowing, or what might be termed "pathetic irony," when Annie appeases her two contending playmates by promising she will be a little wife to both. This foreshadowing is an obvious but sure-fire device of which Tennyson seems to have been particularly fond, for it appears in "Aylmer's Field" and later in *Enoch Arden* when Annie's premonition that she will never see her husband again is met with Enoch's bluff vow that he will, at all events, see her.

Another, subtler kind of foreshadowing also plays a part in Tennyson's rendering of the tale. Philip's visit to Annie after her child has died during Enoch's absence is handled as a graphic anticipation in little of the subsequent unfolding of larger events:

'Surely,' said Philip, 'I may see her now,
May be some little comfort'; therefore went,
Past thro' the solitary room in front,
Paused for a moment at an inner door,
Then struck it thrice, and, no one opening,
Enter'd.

These are not gratuitous minutiae, for each detail will have its counterpart in Philip's unobtruding assumption of Enoch's place, his patient courtship, and his repeatedly deferred winning of the bereft Annie. This same effect—something like the pantomime preceding the play—is present when Philip takes leave of Annie at her door after he has declared his love, and more markedly in the description of Enoch's homecoming—so pictorially contrived—in which the fisherman looks through the window at a scene of domestic felicity and then, stifling a cry which "Would shatter all the happiness of the hearth," steals off into the night. Nor is it incidental to the poet's design that in each of the anticipatory scenes cited the dwelling place stands as a central emblem of peace and the heart's desire.

Such examples of the poem's characteristic art as we have been noting indicate just what Tennyson did for the tale Woolner told him. He was, as he would have said, "setting it to verse," which expresses exactly the impression *Enoch Arden* gives of being a story to which poetry has been *applied* rather than one out of which poetry has been made. Thus Walter Bagehot's characterization of *Enoch Arden* as "a splendid accumulation of impossible accessories" seems apt enough. Yet some exception must be made for the fact that the contrast between Annie's two husbands does touch a level deeper than sentimental decoration. Enoch and Philip appear to be antitypes; but, had Tennyson treated them merely as opposites, he would have falsified both Annie's love for the two men and their sympathy and respect for one another. Each in turn suffers the pain of being excluded, and each accepts it because he sees in the other someone able to realize what he himself desires. "Sincerity," taken in its usual sense, is not a relevant criterion of artistic merit; but it does place in sharper focus some of his poem's most solid virtues to relate these two rivals to contending sides of Tennyson's own nature.

Enoch and Philip possess, respectively, the heroic and domestic manifestation of the same qualities. Where Enoch is bold, Philip is persevering; where Enoch's love leads him to overrule his wife's will and to depart from her, Philip's love leads him to yield to Annie's plea to delay their marriage but to remain a helpful presence. Enoch is rough hewn and Philip exceedingly gentle, and we are reminded that their creator was both the author of "O Darling Room" and a man whose language could shock dinner guests and who liked his meat in great wedges. The fisherman seeks his fortune on perilous seas; the miller remains at home and grows rich. For each type Tennyson could draw upon kindred impulses of his own, and in both his life and art we see something of the contradiction of a Hercules tending the distaff. Hence, perhaps, the particular pathos of the scene where Enoch, the outcast whose isolation on "the beauteous hateful isle" has all but deprived him of the very power of speech, stares through the lighted window at a veritable epitome of snug domesticity.

The Poet Laureate knew these two worlds and their separateness, and the way he juxtaposes them—the one marked by yearning awareness, the other comfortably oblivious—though melodramatic, is not without the quality of genuine vision. We may bridle at his deferential attitude toward the "cups and silver on the burnish'd board," and feel that there are higher claims even than "the happiness of the hearth," but the point is that to the outcast Enoch there are not. Tennyson's final reference to Enoch as a "strong heroic soul" is fully earned by the meaning of his renunciation, but a still more illuminating description comes when, as Enoch turns away from Annie's window, he goes "like a thief." We must see this comparison as psychologically as well as graphically apt; for Enoch had come to the verge, albeit inadvertently, of stealing others' happiness. In this circumstance, self-disclosure would be a crime and so his very identity becomes a burden. If Tennyson sanctifies the tranquility of the hearth, he suggests as well the cost of such a general good in particular repressions and repudiations of the self.

II The Princess

Though a much less "perfect" poem than *Enoch Arden, The Princess* is a considerably more interesting one. Tennyson was never satisfied with it, his admirers have generally been made uncomfortable by it, and it seldom receives much attention in the classroom. Its place as an accomplished poet's first long work has put it at a disadvantage. Were it possible, however, to imagine *The Princess* as, let us say, a newly discovered poem by an anonymous Victorian, we might see it for the odd but remarkable performance it is.

The appearance of *The Princess* in 1847 was a strange answer to the rising hope of reviewers and friends that Tennyson would bring forth a large-scale work. He and Emily Sellwood had discussed the idea for it as early as 1839,[10] and Tennyson believed the story to be quite original. It is told as a "tale from mouth to mouth" by seven members of a college "set" gathered at Vivian-place. Far from the grandly conceived and sustained work many of Tennyson's readers had awaited, *The Princess* is, as its sub-title proclaims, "A Medley"—in its manner of telling, but also in its conglomeration of styles and subjects and in its variety of modern themes in an anachronistic Medieval setting. The elements that the tale itself comprises are adumbrated in the "Prologue," then sorted out again in the "Conclusion" after having been transmitted in the central narrative much as actual experience is refashioned in a dream. The "Prologue" and "Conclusion" that provide a frame of romanticized contemporaneousness and the six intercalary songs (added in 1850) link the poem in tone and form to the English idyls.

As Tennyson's term "medley" describes the form of his out-sized idyl, so his phrase "mock-heroic gigantesque" characterizes its manner. And in that connection W. P. Ker's reference to *The Princess* as "a modern counterpart to *The Rape of the Lock*" [11] offers itself with a good deal of justice. Tennyson, like Pope, is making fun of feminine illusions and, at the same time, tendering a gallant compliment to true femininity. But to pursue the comparison is to discover that Tennyson's way of seeking to accomplish this most delicate double purpose was inherently less suitable than that of his Augustan predecessor. To begin with, *The Princess* employs first-person narrative, with each of the seven who take up the tale becoming "hero in his turn"; and thus the degree of detachment essential to the mock-heroic effect, and one so carefully maintained in Pope's satire, can never be achieved.

A still greater difficulty lies in the fact that in *The Princess* the heroic element is made literal within the context of the narrative. That is to say, the actions and characters are not merely *treated* heroically as in *The Rape of the Lock;* they *are* heroic. Pope's Belinda remains an English coquette though described as if she were a goddess, a victor in battle, and a victim of epic ravishment; Tennyson's Ida is truly the princess of a Medieval never-land that the narrators represent her to be, and thus the social realities being satirized are not solidly depicted but are present only by vague inference. Consequently, Pope's attitude toward his subject strikes us as complex; and Tennyson's seems only confused. Perhaps this difference reflects the diverse temperaments of the two poets and the social temper of dissimilar ages. Pope could put woman in her place because he was sure what her place was; Tennyson was not sure, though he had sentiments on the subject. As a result, his satire is ultimately halfhearted, and his praise tends to cloy.

Even so, the poem's mock heroics, especially in the early sections, are often delightful;[12] but to get at its vital center we must approach *The Princess* from a slightly different direction. Essentially, like *The Rape of the Lock,* the subject of *The Princess* is sexuality. To say so is to refer not simply to the plot of romantic love or to the theme of women's rights, but to the poem's underlying concern with the principal characters' discovery and acceptance of their own sexual natures.[13] The romantic love story and the issue of women's rights both reach their resolutions in the Prince's long conciliatory speech to Princess Ida in Part VII:

> 'The woman's cause is man's; they rise or sink
> Together,
> . . . .
> For woman is not undevelopt man,
> But diverse. Could we make her as the man,
> Sweet Love was slain; his dearest bond is this,
> Not like to like, but like in difference.'

Even at such a moment we see the question of feminism carried beyond the merely social sphere and becoming framed in psychosexual terms.

The story might be characterized as tracing the complementary movements of the Princess toward true femininity and the Prince toward true masculinity. The Prince is described in the first lines of Part I as "like a girl," and his assumption, along with his friends Cyril and Florian, of "female gear" is the dramatic expression of this girlishness. We are told that so disguised the three young men were "a sight to shake/The midriff of despair with laughter," but in fact little hilarity is wrung from the situation, and to the Prince's taunting foes it is a case of "like to like": "The woman's garment hid the woman's heart." In the eyes of Arac's cohorts or the Princc's own bluff father, it is simply a matter of effeminacy: the Prince must "make yourself a man to fight with men." But this view oversimplifies the character of the Prince. After his identity has been exposed, he assures the Princess that he is "not a scorner of your sex/But venerator." However, his veneration has led him to attempt to win Ida by disguising his sexuality rather than by asserting it. The Prince's female garb, then, is not the sign of a pansy so much as that of an idolater of women.

The Prince's infatuation and the surrounding circumstances are presented in illuminating detail. "Alone," he tells the Princess, "from earlier than I know,/Immersed in rich foreshadowings of the world,/I loved the woman" (VII, 292–94). This devotion to woman—a powerful force for good in man, according to the Prince—did not remain for him a generalized or abstract attachment. "Yet there was one," he explains, "thro' whom I loved her [womankind]": his mother. What we have here is something very much like C. G. Jung's conception of the collective image of woman in the male unconscious becoming actualized by projection on to the mother.[14] And also as in Jung, this female image—the *anima*—is subsequently identified with other women, or in this case with a single woman: Princess Ida.

But even before he has set eyes upon the Princess (the pair had been "proxy-wedded" in childhood), the Prince carries her picture next his heart. Thus, for the Prince, Ida is an inner picture before she is a real woman. "My nurse would tell me of you," he reveals to the Princess: "I babbled for you, as babies for the moon,/Vague brightness" (IV, 407–409). The point here, of course, is the relation between "ideal" and real woman. The Prince's female idolatry, fixed upon his mother and then upon Ida's picture, projects itself in the form of woman as an unassailable paragon. His "weird seizures" testify to the contradictions and frustrations inherent in this desire to possess the unattainable. In this sense Ida, the beautiful and imperious amazon, functions not only as an example of woman's will to "lift her nature up," but as the externalization of the Prince's *anima*.

However, the barrier to love is in Ida even more evident than in the Prince. As he conceals his masculinity, so she denies her femininity. We can see in the two of them an illustration of the Jungian contention that the *anima* produces *moods* (the Prince's seizures) whereas the *animus*—the masculine element in woman—produces *opinions* (the precepts to which the Princess so staunchly clings). Against this opinionated mind female instinct at length prevails. The object that initially arouses the woman in Ida is, appropriately enough, a child—Lady Psyche's little girl; and in ministering to the Prince after he is wounded in the fight to win her, Ida moves fully in her "own clear element."

Jung's psychology commonly interprets the child as a symbol of the self. Aglaia, the little girl, has something of this function; certainly, in softening her woman's heart toward Psyche's daughter, Ida is accepting a part of her own nature that she had repelled and so approaches true selfhood. Such selfhood is, in fact, the goal both the Princess and the Prince finally reach and the condition their union signifies. Ida's aim, for herself and her sex, in establishing her college and in espousing the feminist cause is seemingly identical with the goal of selfhood. But, whereas she exhorts her followers to "lift your natures up," the better course in her own case is expresed in the "small sweet idyl" she reads the stricken Prince: "Come down, O maid, from yonder mountain height." "Love is of the valley," the idyl says; and this descent involves a change in Ida from feminist to female. It is not, however, a reversal of values but rather a matter of discrimination and discovery. Early in the poem the Princess voices her contempt for the pretense of conventionalized love poems, applying herself to the composition of "awful odes" on more solemn subjects. But after a kiss has brought her the taste of passion and "Her falser self slipt from her like a robe,/And left her woman," Ida's reading of the delicately erotic "Now sleeps the crimson petal" exhibits a different sort of love poetry and her newly gained capacity to respond to it.

The Prince's progress toward selfhood requires that he exert his manliness without assuming the brute masculinity of his father. It is significant that the man beneath the woman's garb is first revealed when he strikes Cyril for singing a tavern catch "unmeet for ladies." Yet his later refusal to suspect Cyril capable of anything dishonorable and his reconciliation with him are more manful still. As the Prince reveals his full nature, he seems increasingly disposed to grant woman hers. He reminds his father that women cannot be carelessly lumped together but "have as many differences as we"; and he acknowledges in woman a wholeness lacking in "the piebald miscellany, man"—all this culminating in the Prince's tribute to "distinctive womanhood" in Part VII. Veneration has matured to genuine appreciation.

The poem's lesser characters elaborate its basic theme. The two fathers are contrasting types whose failings are inversely mirrored in the reactions of their children: Gama, "A little dry old man . . . /Not like a king," leaves the impression that Ida is a victim not of too much masculine authority but of too little; the Prince's father, on the other hand, "thought a king a king." If anything can make the Prince's effeminacy at all endurable, his father's overbearing view that "Man is the hunter; woman is his game" does so. To each of his principals Tennyson assigns a pair of associates who act somewhat as embodiments of antithetical sides of both the Prince's and the Princess's characters. Florian and Cyril, the courtly "half-self" and the impulsive and faintly disreputable crony, correspond to the more and the less flattering truths about himself such a man must face.[15] The two widows, Lady Blanche and Psyche, dramatize the matriarchal and the maternal inclinations that contend in Ida.

Against this series of oppositions the Prince and Princess, in taking possession of each other and of their true selves, represent unity and wholeness. The Prince tells Ida "either sex alone/Is half itself," and the two look toward a time when "The man [will] be more of woman, she of man." But clearly this ideal is the reward not of repressing sexuality but of accepting it. Tennyson puts the negative side of the matter thus in an epigram, "On One Who Affected an Effeminate Manner":

> While man and woman still are incomplete,
> I prize that soul where man and woman meet,
> Which types all Nature's male and female plan,
> But, friend, man-woman is not woman-man.

In *The Princess* he is more positive. It is a remarkable point for a Victorian poem to make that sex—which, viewed falsely, separates man and woman—is really the means of overcoming its own barrier: a way, in the aptness of the biblical usage, to *know* another.

And hence a way to know oneself. The Prince's proposal to Ida of a union in which she shall "Accomplish thou my manhood and thyself" (VII, 344) confirms their relationship as neither a jealousy-ridden contest nor a degrading idol worship, but as an enterprise for mutual fulfillment and self-knowledge. Tennyson's lovers aspire to a state much like what Jung means by "individuation": they are reconciled with seemingly diverse elements that constitute their natures; the wholeness of each is not a separation from but an integration with life beyond one's own. As serene and resolute, with the world all before them, as Milton's Adam and Eve, only with no taint of shame or regret, the Prince and Princess stand ready to reclaim "the statelier Eden":

> all the past
> Melts mist-like into this bright hour, and this
> Is morn no more.

. . . .
O, we will walk this world,
Yoked in all exercise of noble end.'
(VII, 333–35; 339–40)

III *The* Idylls of the King

When we add to Tennyson's almost lifelong absorption in the legends of King Arthur the persistent yet unfulfilled claim this subject had made upon English poets since Spenser and the ubiquitous neo-Gothicism of his own time, the *Idylls of the King* seems the all but fated result. Between the time, shortly after Arthur Hallam's death in 1833, when Tennyson began writing *Morte d'Arthur*, and 1874, when he completed "*Balin* and *Balan*," stretches the span of the work's actual genesis; the twelve idylls were not published together in their established order, however, until 1889. Through half a lifetime, then, Tennyson was at least to some degree occupied with his Arthurian epic: studying his sources, collecting impressions of authentic scenery, making prose paraphrases, composing and revising, wrenching the accumulating tales toward some kind of unity and—not least—chafing under the burden of an unfinished task. What wonder if the task became at times less a compelling vision than a nagging duty? Yet the *Idylls of the King*, which Tennyson's contemporaries regarded as the crown of his career and quickly installed as a schoolroom staple, remains—any fair-minded and reasonably discerning encounter with the poem makes clear—not simply a monument to Victorian bad taste and the Laureate's perseverance. Though it gives us much cause for dissatisfaction, the *Idylls* also gives us a major poet in the fullest, most mature possession of his powers. And, for whatever the distinction may be worth, it is probably the last heroic poem in our language.

There is a point in taking such classifications as "heroic poem" seriously; for, until we recognize the kind of work we are dealing with, we can neither understand nor evaluate it properly. One of the most serious and persistent criticisms leveled against Tennyson's *Idylls* is that by infusing Arthurian story with nineteenth-century attitudes and values and by imposing upon it his own moral vision, Tennyson is guilty of an inexcusable anachronism. Swinburne's jest about "le Morte d'Albert," Hopkins's reference to

Medieval charades, and George Meredith's remark that Arthur talks like a curate, all reflect this point of view; and it is common to most of the dispraise the *Idylls* has subsequently suffered.

But the anachronism of heroic poetry is one of its essential, as well as one of its traditional elements; it has the effect of both venerating the present and modernizing the past. Homer's Troy is not quite the one Schliemann rediscovered; the piety of Aeneas is no reconstruction of ancient modes of behavior, real or imagined, but the conscious celebration of a prime Augustan virtue; and *The Faerie Queene* is approximately as Elizabethan as Tennyson's *Idylls* is Victorian. Thus when Frederic Harrison complained of "the incongruity of making belted knights with fairy mothers talking modern morality," [16] he was not so much scoring a point against the *Idylls of the King* as denying the validity of that kind of poetry to which it belongs.

Moreover, the charge that Tennyson's attempt to accommodate the code of Medieval *amour courtois* to Victorian moral standards constitutes "a fundamental tactical error" [17] assumes a view of his material that Tennyson cannot be expected to have shared. To him, moral degeneration had been the fate as well as the subject of the Arthurian romances; Courtly Love was commonly held to have been a perversion of what Ernest Renan, who discussed Celtic legend with Tennyson on numerous occasions, termed the "virginal modesty" of the original Breton romances.[18] When Hallam Tennyson describes how his father "made the old legends his own" by adding to them "a spirit of modern thought and an ethical significance," he also claims that their "idealism" was "restored." [19] To be sure, the result may sometimes strike us as mere respectability thinly disguised. But Tennyson would not have understood the inference that disguise was intended or necessary, and he cannot really be blamed for supposing that the moral assumptions he accepted in life and the ideal of conduct he discovered in Arthurian legend were in essential accord.

Tennyson's chivalry, in fact, *deliberately* places the stress upon external manners, or—more fairly and more accurately—upon the relation between outward behavior and inward virtue. Indeed, the concept of chivalry suggested to the Victorian mind the distillation of its own convictions respecting the importance of social propriety as at once the necessary condition and the outward sign of the more intrinsic spiritual graces. So much is indicated by Sir

Edward Strachey's discussion of the subject in his introduction to Malory's *Morte d'Arthur* published in 1868: "There is truth in the old motto, 'Manners makyth man.' Manners, like laws, create a region and atmosphere of virtue within which all good more easily lives and grows and evil finds it harder to maintain itself. . . . But manners are good not only as affording a fairer field for the exercise of the higher virtues, but good in themselves. They are a real part of the beauty and grace of our human life."[20]

The *Idylls of the King* advances a similar claim regarding the externality of the chivalrous ideal. The vows of conduct to which Arthur swears his knights are a crucial civilizing force in themselves, giving shape and direction as they do to an innate decency. But, more than that, they represent a visible manifestation of the "higher virtues." In *In Memoriam* (CXI) Tennyson had praised "noble manners" as "the flower/And native growth of noble mind"; Arthur, in "Guinevere," echoes this sentiment: "For manners are not idle, but the fruit/Of loyal nature and of noble mind." (ll. 333–34)." Chivalry, throughout the *Idylls,* stands not so much for an antiquated code as for that "atmosphere of virtue" which is true civility in any society in any age.

Rather than resting smugly upon this connection of manners to virtue, however, the poem conceives the relationship as most precarious. Manners may be the manifestation of virtue, but they can also be its spurious imitation or even the masquerade of vice. In idealizing civility Tennyson creates a natural perspective from which to consider the characteristic perils such an ideal risks: superficiality, envy, hypocrisy and self-deceit, and ultimate cynicism or disillusionment. The relationship of King Arthur and his chief knight Lancelot is the focal point of this theme, though numerous variations radiate from it. Here the distinction between inward strength of conscience and essential excellence, on the one hand, and outward courtesy and formal accomplishment, on the other, is dramatized—"For Lancelot was first in the tournament,/But Arthur mightiest on the battle-field," ("Gareth and Lynette," ll. 485–86).

Arthur, whom critics have rightly regarded as "colorless," is, at least in terms of his thematic function, properly so. His moral substance is shadowed forth in the world of appearance—in the jousts, even in his courtly service to the Queen—by Lancelot. But, as the sun's pure radiance is the source of all color, so Lancelot owes his true nobility to his love of King Arthur and to his loyalty to his vows. Thus Guinevere's unfaithfulness is a case of mistaking appearance for reality; as she herself partly realizes, her fascination for the refracted light Lancelot emits is a love of the *good* that blinds her to the *best*. "Who can gaze upon the sun in heaven?" she asks. "Who loves me must have a touch of earth;/The low sun makes the colour" ("Lancelot and Elaine," ll. 123, 133–34). Lancelot's external graces are real enough, they are even essential to the working of the King's will; but they are susceptible to being taken for the all-in-all and thus become a tragic gift.

Considering the piecemeal manner in which the *Idylls of the King* grew toward the twelve parts that tradition—on the Virgilian model—makes proper, Tennyson's epic contains surprising and impressive elements of unity. Though it flirts with the allegorical, the work can not be read as a consistent allegory; but Tennyson's own claim of a "parabolic drift" to the poem is both an accurate and a useful description of the quality from which emerge certain unifying patterns. In the envoy "To the Queen," Tennyson refers to his poem as "shadowing Sense at war with Soul/Ideal manhood closed in real man"; and, in a general way, Arthur does represent man's higher nature—"soul" or "conscience"—striving to bring into existence and sustain an order, a harmony, but beset by the natural tendencies and active antagonisms of the baser self.

This conflict is reiterated within single characters such as Balin, Pelleas, and Lancelot and through polar characters, some of whom are dramatically juxtaposed (Merlin and Vivien) and some only thematically contrasted (Elaine and Etarre). Moreover, it is framed within the compass of human life, Arthur's coming and his passing furnishing the subjects of the first and last idyll. The seasonal cycle gives its elemental rhythm to this recurring pageant of a glorious but doomed contention with the mortal frailties. For, in one dimension, Arthur is a solar hero; Tennyson arranged the *Idylls* and designed its various moods and weathers to follow the seasons, from the springtime of the King's marriage to the winter of his discontent; and the poet concludes the whole on a note of minimal cheer by accompanying Arthur's passing with the sunrise of a new year.

The cycle of twelve idylls does not, of course, constitute a coherent narrative, but against the background of seasonal decline unfold the steadily worsening consequences of a corrupting evil. It is obvious that Tennyson alleges a direct causal connection between the disloyal love of Lancelot and Queen Guinevere and the weakening and dissolution of Arthur's Order; but the connection is more effective on the symbolic than on the realistic level. The poem's truest concern is not the consequences of domestic infidelity but the erosion of innocence, confidence, and a sense of ethical stability by suspicion, cynicism, and moral nihilism. Moving from idyll to idyll, we watch, sometimes at a far remove, sometimes close at hand, the working out of an infection amidst a stricken society—except that "infection" connotes an abnormal condition, whereas what Tennyson envisions has about it almost the inevitability of natural process.

"The Coming of Arthur," which was added in 1869, serves to impose the symbolic framework upon the sequence of idylls. It concerns Arthur's marriage to Guinevere and, by means of the incorporated narratives of Bedivere and Bellicent, his dubious origin. Here the King's significance as man's spiritual part, "ideal manhood," and the human conscience is established. The uncertainties regarding his claim to rightful authority represent the inherent status of an essentially spiritual view of man. Bedivere's account of Arthur's origin is circumstantial, Bellicent's is visionary; and, though both believe him to be the true king, it is to the accompaniment of Leodogran's vexed questionings "whether there were truth in anything" and Merlin's agnostic riddlings: "Sun, rain, and sun! and where is he who knows?/From the great deep to the great deep he goes." (ll. 409–10). Man's coming hither and his going hence, so Tennyson affirmed, are a mystery; and no less so is his spirituality. Arthur's legitimacy must rest upon the proof of what he *does* and upon the faith of those whose vows bestow upon them the king's "momentary likeness." Even then, as Leodogran's dream portends, Arthur's kingship can be fully acknowledged only in heaven.

Arthur's kingly prowess, which is as manifest as his origin is obscure, finds expression in the solar analogy. Born with the new year, he is hailed by his knighthood at his wedding as "our Sun . . . mighty in his May." His power is described as lightening the dead land, making the dead world live, "Letting in the sun." The marriage with Guinevere similarly has overtones of a cosmic harmony of sun and earth, but more explicit is its significance as a kind of "soul/body" relationship. Guinevere is characterized as "fairest of all flesh on earth," and her function is described as a complement to the King's spirituality, completing or giving substance to it while being ennobled by it in turn: "Shall I not lift her from this land of beasts/Up to my throne and side by side with me? . . . asks Arthur of the beautiful daughter of Leodogran; ". . . for saving I be join'd/To her that is the fairest under heaven,/I seem as nothing in the mighty world" (ll. 84–86). There is a sense in which the *Idylls of the King* is thus a tragic variation on the theme of sexuality as fulfillment, which Tennyson had treated idyllically in *The Princess.*

Though the King's might exerts itself abroad in the world, its hold upon men—as exemplified by the Order of the Round Table —is an inward force. In this aspect it is distinguished from those polar forces against which Arthur gains his initial triumphs: "Rome" and "Heathen," the latter subject to no higher comprehension and the former a type of external dogmatic authority. Arthur's knights, on the other hand, are sworn "To reverence the King, as if he were/Their conscience, and their conscience as their King ("Guinevere," 465–66)." It is from this new principle and the dignity it gives the individual by making "Man's word . . . God in man" that the King and his Order derive moral energy and political legitimacy. Thus Arthur refuses to become a tributary of Rome, "The slowly-fading mistress of the world," advising her emissaries that "The old order changeth, yielding place to new." The words foreshadow their more famous context in the last idyll and establish the cyclic cast of the entire epic's imaginative world.

In the next ten idylls, collectively designated "The Round Table," Arthur stands more as a moral gauge than as a dramatic figure. "Gareth and Lynette," the first of these, though marred somewhat by rather heavy word play and other mannered touches in the dialogue, such as Tennyson often affects whenever he tries for a Shakespearean gusto, does exude a proper vernal charm. As befits a springtime idyll, the story concerns Gareth's coming into manhood by casting free from the benign snares of a protective mother and by changing the fair Lynette's scorn to love as his deeds reveal the knightly qualities concealed beneath the guise of a kitchen knave. Camelot, too, is in its prime as a seat of innocence and virtue; Arthur's radiance as a "Sun of Glory" is as yet unclouded by any disloyalty or whispered scandal. Indeed, Lancelot figures in this idyll as Gareth's model of the true knight; and the younger champion's use of Lancelot's shield and charger in his final test symbolizes the attainment of essential knighthood. Malice within the realm assumes only the mildest form in the peripheral figure of Kay the senechal, whereas the falseness of a Mark is exposed and confounded with the utmost ease.

At this point in the epic, the emphasis given the true-false theme is upon the emergence of the "true" from a rather readily displaced falsity. The wicked or the base, not to mention the merely misconceived, is but a foil for the genuine and the good. A recurrent imagery in "Gareth and Lynette" of fire bursting from smoke or ashes epitomizes this theme. Reality does not lie in unpromising appearances but in the heart: "The knave that doth thee service as full knight/Is all as good, meseems, as any knight" (ll. 991–92). And, in "the war of Time against the soul of man," which Gareth reenacts with his four allegorical adversaries, the awesome armor of Death conceals only "the bright face of a blooming boy."

Tennyson finds in paradox the natural mode for expressing the affirmations that dominate "Gareth and Lynette." By disguising his nobility Gareth reveals it; by courting a lady's scorn he wins her love: "So Gareth all for glory underwent/The sooty yoke of kitchen-vassalage" (ll. 468–69). The essence of this optimistic vision—challenged, overborne, and finally vindicated, though radically tempered, in subsequent idylls—appears in Lancelot's words: "Thrown have I been, nor once, but many a time./Victor from vanquish'd issues at the last/And overthrower from being overthrown" (ll. 1229–31). The archetypal paradox such statements affirm: "What is not, *is*," furnishes the rhetorical—and poetic—strategy for saying "yes" to life.

This strategy is still operative in the two idylls that follow: "The Marriage of Geraint" and "Geraint and Enid." Geraint dons rusty armor to do shining deeds; Enid, compelled to wear a dingy gown, emerges from the shadow of her husband's suspicions clothed, literally and figuratively, like "the sun in heaven." The traitorous Edyrn admits to Geraint "By overthrowing me you threw me higher. . . . There was I broken down, there was I saved." But in this pair of idylls (originally composed as one) falseness has become somewhat more formidable. To mistake falsity for truth begins to seem more inherent in the nature of things; the gap has perceptibly narrowed between the ideal world of the poem and the real and imperfect world of the poet.

The flaw that has revealed itself is suspiciousness. Presumably the Queen's "guilty love for Lancelot" precedes the "world's loud whisper" which poisons Geraint's trust in his own wife, but the poem's scale of moral priorities places almost more initial blame upon distrust and trafficking in rumors of wrongdoing than upon the wrong itself. Geraint is at fault in letting the possibility of corruption render him at once morally impotent and rigidly severe; but, though Shakespeare could draw from a similar situation endless complexities, Tennyson's hero is no Hamlet. These idylls most clearly illustrate Tennyson's lack of subtlety and finesse in characterization, more particularly the meagerness of his powers of empathy. It is hard, in fact, to dissent from Harold Nicolson's conclusion that "Geraint is a cad and Enid a noodle." [21]

In "Balin and Balan" the atmosphere has darkened. Imagery in the Geraint idylls pictures the sun breaking through clouds, but in "Balin and Balan" the pattern of light and shadow implies less optimism. The perils have grown more tenebrous yet more persistent. Out of the dark, arrows and spears fly from unseen hands; vice is hidden in the recesses of the self or lurks in the secrets of deceit and shadows of scandal. Buried in deep woods too lies the gloomy hall of the ascetic Pellam, too other-worldly to keep his word; for in this last-written of the idylls Tennyson wishes to draw spiritual fanaticism into counterpoise with its contrasting evil, sensuality, in thematic support and anticipation of "The Holy Grail."

Balin, seeking to curb his "violence" by true courtesy, emulates Lancelot's devotion to the Queen; but now Lancelot is a false model, and Balin's near-despair at his high example becomes the fury of disillusionment as he is worked upon by the scorn of Garlon, "shadow" and "ghost," and the "sunnily" smiling Vivien. It is the crowning irony in this interplay of light and shadow that the falseness of a Vivien should arrogate to itself the sunny naturalness of brute instinct. Her song proclaims, in the accents of a Swinburnian neo-paganism, a recrudescence of the "old sun-worship":

'The fire of heaven is lord of all things good,
And starve not thou this fire within thy blood,
But follow Vivien thro' the fiery flood!
The fire of heaven is not the flame of hell!'
(ll. 446–49)

Naturalism, then, challenges Arthur's spirituality dressed in similar imagery and offering itself, similarly, as the truest reflection of man's essential nature. But the dark ending of "Balin and Balan" illuminates the crucial difference. Vivien sees in the twin deaths of Balin and Balan only folly and waste. Her squire supposes that those who die for love might be happy, but Vivien mocks at such illusions: "I better prize/The living dog than the dead lion" (ll. 573–74). This realism, however, has its own blindness; there is an alternate view. The tragedy, though purposeless, is mitigated by the brothers' mutual affirmation of their filial bond in a spirit truly illustrative of Milton's "calm of mind all passion spent." Their lives are not triumphant, but they die well.

Vivien, "born from death," confirmed in hate—and the antithesis of all the King stands for ("as Arthur in the highest/Leaven'd the world, so Vivien in the lowest")—becomes a central figure in the next idyll ("Merlin and Vivien"). In the manner of Milton's Satan, she has taken evil to be her good and can see even in Arthur's goodness only the cause of Lancelot and Guinevere's crime. Since Merlin and Vivien are somewhat like polarized simplifications of Arthur and Guinevere, there may be some justification in Tennyson's having cast this idyll almost in the form of a Body/Soul *débat*. However, the result is a poem whose lack of incident and real drama makes it one of the least successful of the *Idylls*.

"Lancelot and Elaine," though also one of the original four idylls, makes a marked contrast with "Merlin and Vivien," which it follows in the final arrangement. Tennyson delighted to read aloud the tale of the "lily maid of Astolat," and this idyll has been much admired for its "tender touches." Even when the tenderness palls, much remains to indicate that Tennyson was not wholly without a flair for narrative. The fundamental opposition between a touching innocence and the sorrowful complexities of experience could always engage him strongly. Also he makes the most of such particular contrasts as those between the wistful, sacrificing love of Elaine and the jealous and guilty passion of Guinevere, and between the manners of the marred but noble Lancelot and the tinkling courtesies of Gawain. We endure more readily the "lily maid" sections of the poem because they are intermixed with the more resonant passages concerned with the Queen and her paramour.

Tennyson embroiders the story with many a scene typical of his decorative approach to narrative. Lancelot and Lavaine draw towards the lists and behold Arthur presiding over the tournament, as sumptuously posed as a Pre-Raphaelite design. To his admiring young companion Lancelot confides:

> '. . . in me there dwells
> No greatness, save it be some far-off touch
> Of greatness to know well I am not great.
> There is the man.'
> (ll. 447–50)

The whole scene is richly wrought: the regal figure of Arthur, Lancelot's poignant sense of his inherent inferiority to the King he has betrayed, and the ambiguous echo of the biblical *ecce homo,* which even as it proclaims Arthur's Christ-like majesty reverberates with parallels to Pilate's hypocrisy and the mockery of the crown of thorns. Though we are unaccustomed to identify cuckoldry with martyrdom, Tennyson in this instance gets away with it. It is all a matter of context; there is nothing intrinsically appropriate, either, in the connection between apple stealing and original sin.

In "Lancelot and Elaine" the theme of true and false takes an interesting turn. The simple disguises of earlier idylls now become more pervasive and complex. Concealment assumes many forms: Lancelot conceals his identity in order to win greater glory; Guinevere, her jealousy; Gawain, his disloyalty; and Elaine, her love. Lancelot's situation is reversed from what it was in "Gareth and Lynette," where his shield helps the untried knight to prove himself. Now Lancelot must borrow the blank shield of Sir Torre; and, wearing Elaine's favor in the tourney, he actually contends with his own reputation, which his kin struggle to uphold against this stronger knight. Thus, in reenacting true knighthood as the champion of the innocent Elaine, Lancelot is at enmity with himself.

But still more significant is the way "truth" may become the tool of falseness. Guinevere uses Arthur's "passionate perfection" as an excuse for her own derelictions. "He is all fault who hath no fault at all," she argues.[22] In another sense, too, the true is perverted to serve false ends. Lancelot cannot avail himself of the saving love of Elaine because his virtue, tainted though it is, will not allow him to be disloyal to his Queen: "The shackles of an old love straiten'd him,/His honour rooted in dishonour stood,/ And faith unfaithful kept him falsely true." (ll. 870–72). Paradox, which had governed the earlier *Idylls,* has in this flourish of oxymorons modulated into irony.

Tennyson undertook the subject of "The Holy Grail" reluctantly; for, as he explained to the Duke of Argyll, "It would be too much like playing with sacred things. The old writers *believed* in the Sangreal." [23] However, he met this difficulty by having Sir Percivale, whose faith is certainly sufficient for the task, relate the story to his fellow monk, Ambrosius. This narrative strategy is, beyond that, an effective means by which the poet's own ambivalent attitude toward the quest can be maintained. For only if the disastrous enthusiasm of the Round Table is told with the reverence of a Percivale can it stand as the piece of noble folly that Tennyson's conception requires. As he interprets it, the Grail Quest presents the issue of spiritual fervor in relation to practical virtue. For the bulk of Arthur's Order, the truest opportunity to lose themselves in a saving cause lies near at hand in noble deeds; to seek the Grail, which only Galahad claims actually to have seen, is but to "follow wandering fires."

Though a social calamity, the Quest is not simply a fool's errand. For each knight, in his degree, it is at least a self-discovery. Percivale's own quest acts out the universal spiritual pilgrimage; the saintly Galahad achieves some kind of ultimate transcendence; Bors, truehearted and selfless, is vouchsafed a sight of the Grail he scarcely sought for himself; to Lancelot, maddened by the quest, comes the cheerless insight that his very nobility of mind insures his suffering: "Happier are those that welter in their sin,/Swine in the mud, that cannot see for slime" (ll. 767–68). Arthur's bitter sense of what the Grail Quest has cost, then, must be distinguished from the "reckless and innocent" contempt of Gawain. Arthur reproves him as "Being too blind to have desire to see"—a worse blunder than affected mysticism.

Misguided though the enterprise has been, it only confirms the sorrowing King's confidence that "This air that smites his [*i.e.*, man's] forehead is not air/But vision" (ll. 910–11).

Though "Pelleas and Ettarre" is frequently dismissed as one of the weakest links in Tennyson's Arthuriad—a ridiculous story about an overstrained youth which hardly deserves such solemn and elaborate rendering—it makes, in fact, an important contribution to the working out of the larger themes and merits more interest than commentators have seemed to allow it. Its place is as a more unsparing exploration of the course of disillusionment, found earlier in "Balin and Balan," and as a dissonant echo of "Gareth and Lynette." Pelleas encounters falseness more starkly and at closer range than does Balin. Balin's illusions as to the Queen's purity are restored by his brother as he dies; Pelleas has neither death nor delusion to relieve his abject and smoldering impotence. Like Gareth, Pelleas has the youth and the *joie de vivre* to persevere against a maiden's scorn; but, whereas in Gareth's green world bravery and steadfastness win the prize of love, Pelleas earns only Ettarre's contempt; and, rather than proving himself, he is borne down by futility and self-disgust. In "Gareth and Lynette," Lancelot is a true model of courtesy for the young knight; in "Pelleas and Ettarre," this function has degenerated into Gawain's treacherous substitution for Pelleas. With Lancelot's shield, Gareth prevails; lending Gawain his armor to court Ettarre in his behalf, Pelleas is betrayed.

The mode which characterizes "Gareth and Lynette" and the affirmative emphasis of the other idylls in the ascendant part of the cycle is paradox—"What is not, *is*." In "Pelleas and Ettarre," irony, which has crept into earlier idylls in various forms, becomes fully dominant. As paradox is the strategy of affirmation, irony is the strategy of negation—"What is, *is not*." [24] The ironic tone is set when Pelleas, exclaiming over his as yet unencountered beloved, speaks of her as "pure as Guinevere."

Pelleas's subsequent discovery that Ettarre and Guinevere are both false drives him to depths of disillusionment that, if judged in a literalistic framework, do seem almost childishly extreme. But Pelleas is in the tradition of romantic heroes, and Ettarre is his "epipsyche," the incarnation of his subjective ideal: ". . . so did Pelleas lend/ All the young beauty of his own soul to hers" (ll. 78–79). Thus the disillusionment of Pelleas is of a significantly different order from that of Balin. His discovery of Ettarre and Gawain bedded together is followed by an illuminating description of his reaction:

> Back, as a coward slinks from what he fears
> To cope with, or a traitor proven, or hound
> Beaten, did Pelleas in an utter shame
> Creep with his shadow thro' the court again.
> (ll. 429–32)

Curiously, the wronged one responds as if he were himself guilty of the wrongdoing. The clear implication is that the "shame" attaches itself to Pelleas, because to him the scene is a revelation of the "truth" about his own ideal. Having taken Ettarre's beauty for the objectification of his soul's purity, Pelleas now finds in her lewdness a reflection of his own essential vileness. Gawain, his surrogate, "betrays" Pelleas in the sense not only of violating his trust, but also of ironically disclosing—by acting out—the real nature of his own desires: "I never loved her, I but lusted for her" (l. 475).

Pelleas's fit of self-contempt leads him to denounce any human pretense to live by ideals—most particularly Arthur's Order and the vows:

> 'Love?—we be all alike; only the King
> Hath made us fools and liars. O noble vows!
> O great and sane and simple race of brutes
> That own no lust because they have no law!'
> (ll. 469–72)

This is a kind of moral primitivism which, reduced to its essence, argues that to have no principles of conduct is morally superior to affirming principles that cannot be followed. In the next idyll, "The Last Tournament," such a reduction has grown virtually into a rival ideology. It is overtly espoused by the Red Knight, whose Round Table in the North is the ironic counterpart of Arthur's:

> 'The vow that binds too strictly snaps itself—
> My knighthood taught me this—ay, being snapt—
> We run more counter to the soul thereof
> Than had we never sworn.'
> (ll. 652–55)

The tournament itself, to which the title of the idyll refers, is named with blatant enough irony: The Tournament of the Dead Innocence. Suggestive of the moral climate, Arthur is absent; in his stead, Lancelot presides, a fitting substitute at this travesty of chivalry. He watches in "languorous mood" as the rules of the tournament are broken and "gibes and flickering mockeries" mark the scene. In the tourney's victor, Tristram, we see, if Lancelot does not, the exaggerated image of his own worst self. Trueheartedness resides only in Dagonet, the King's fool; somewhat like his literary ancestor the Fool in *King Lear*, he underscores a condition of rampant vice in which virtue is driven to assume the guise of folly.

Tennyson employs the Tristram and Isolt story as an ironic reduction of the Arthur-Guinevere-Lancelot triangle. Arthur's gentleness of spirit and guilelessness are slanderously parodied in the craven, feckless Mark. But the very qualities Tristram and Isolt scorn in the man they have wronged make him deadly: he steals out of the dark to cleave the skull of the defenseless Tristram. Even before that finishing stroke, however, the two lovers have reached the dead end of their cynicism: Tristram, when Isolt berates him for having married, banters her: "May God be with thee, sweet, when old and gray,/And past desire!" (ll. 622–23). Isolt's pathetic reply shows "realism" arriving at that point where it confronts the ultimate irony of its own need of illusion:

'Flatter me rather, seeing me so weak,
Broken with Mark and hate and solitude,
Thy marriage and mine own, that I should suck
Lies like sweet wines. Lie to me; I believe.'
(ll. 637–40)

Again the origin of the conception seems Shakespearean; this time the great locus of disenchantment, Sonnet 138, whose final lines Tennyson has fittingly (though without the erotic puns) echoed: "Therefore I lie with her and she with me,/And in our faults by lies we flattered be."

Despite its disjointed narrative elements—the tournament, Arthur's clash with the Red Knight, and the Tristram-Isolt scene—"The Last Tournament" constitutes an impressive evocation of the atmosphere of spiritual atrophy:

The sudden trumpet sounded as in a dream
To ears but half-awaked, then one low roll
Of autumn thunder, and the jousts began;
And ever the wind blew, and the yellowing leaf,
And gloom and gleam, and shower and shorn plume
Went down it. Sighing weariedly, as one
Who sits and gazes on a faded fire,
When all all the goodlier guests are past away,
Sat their great umpire looking o'er the lists.
(ll. 151–59)

In such passages the poem rises quite beyond the reach of belittling references to "medieval charades."

"Guinevere" follows "The Last Tournament," not only in the working out of the corrupting evil and the breaking down of Arthur's Order, but also in giving an answer to the question posed crucially by "The Last Tournament" concerning the view of conduct proper to man's nature. Tristram's arguments and the Red Knight's defiant assertion proclaim the *un*naturalness of Arthur's code of conscience and obedience to laws that restrain the impulses of sense. In "Guinevere" Tennyson counters this naturalistic position with one fairly characterized by Matthew Arnold's admonition: "Man must begin, know this, where Nature ends."[25]

This idyll opens with the Queen's having sought anonymous refuge in cloistered Almesbury. The scandal has broken and Arthur's foes are upon him. A very theatrically conceived piece, the two scenes between Guinevere and the little novice, contrasting garrulous innocence and brooding guilt, are balanced on either side of the central confrontation between Arthur and his fallen Queen. Her lofty imperiousness changes dramatically to abjectness and finally to humility in the course of the poem.

The usual way of treating "Guinevere" is to focus attention upon Arthur's long, cleric-like disquisition on the theme: "Yet must I leave thee, woman, to thy shame," and to deplore such smug, almost brutal self-righteousness as the unpardonable ruination of the poem. There is no denying that parts of this sermon must stick in the craw of any sensitive reader—such as the references to the erring wife "like a new disease" who "poisons half the young," and to the King's very flesh revolted at the "polluted" flesh of Guinevere. Yet, in fairness, it should be noted that Arthur reiterates his love, and that he does think of eternal reunion with

Guinevere as his own "last hope." But more important still is the actual place Arthur's words have in the idyll. Their relation to the change wrought in Guinevere rather than what they are in themselves constitutes such justification as can be claimed for them.

Guinevere is the central figure, and the idyll is a study of her acceptance and understanding of guilt. In the first scene involving the Queen and the simple little novice, Guinevere is lacerated by virtually every word the nun speaks; she is the victim of that irony which makes the words of the innocent a torment to the guilty. This suffering she confuses with true repentance:

> 'But help me, Heaven, for surely I repent!
> For what is true repentance but in thought—
> Not even in inmost thought to think again
> The sins that made the past so pleasant to us?
> And I have sworn never to see him more,
> To see him more.'
>
> (ll. 370–75)

The wistful repetition at the end of this passage reveals her self-deception, and straightway Guinevere's thoughts go "slipping back upon the golden days" of her first love for Lancelot. And she clearly regrets not her wickedness but its exposure. When Arthur has taken leave of her, however, this nostalgia is replaced by hope. The Queen's refrain changes significantly from "too late" to "Is it yet too late?" and her thoughts turn from the first meeting with her lover to the prospect of some eternal reunion with the King. The manifest signs of this more genuine repentance are apt. Guinevere answers Arthur's forgiveness in the only way she can: by forgiving the novice (no doubt some acts of innocence are in need of shame's mercy) and, as the prime regenerative step, by forgiving herself: "I must not scorn myself; he loves me still" (l. 667).

Guinevere's attainment of moral insight involves the repudiation of a false naturalism and a recognition that, as one commentator has succinctly stated, "a morality which merely conforms to our nature is based upon less than the highest possibility of our nature; we are most human when we transcend our ordinary selves." [26]

'I yearn'd for warmth and colour which I found
In Lancelot—now I see thee what thou art,
Thou art the highest and most human too.
. . . .
We needs must love the highest when we see it.'
(ll. 642–44, 655)

With these words the mode of paradox reasserts itself, and a note of tempered affirmation returns to the *Idylls*. Many sensible readers object, of course, that in plain truth Guinevere is mistaken: as compared to Lancelot, the King is not highest and certainly not most human; she has chosen not goodness but weakness.[27] However, it is surely a calculated part of the poem's essential meaning that goodness, in the world of appearances, does look like weakness. In such a world Arthur is indeed "the King of fools," and his ideal manhood can never have the obvious appeal of Lancelot's courtesy. Were this *not* the case, Guinevere's fall would be unforgivable and hence lacking significance; and her repentance could have no more importance than a superficial change of heart.

Nevertheless, we need not approve Tennyson's characterization of Arthur, the wronged husband. In "The Passing of Arthur," however—the last idyll, which Tennyson made by expanding his earliest essay at Arthurian epic, the "Morte d'Arthur"—the King, as stricken champion, makes a better showing. If "Guinevere" fails to sustain the contention that the highest is most human, "The Passing" almost does so. Arthur comes much closer than elsewhere to embodying both the all but ineffable attributes of Soul at war with Sense and the qualities of a tragic hero. Some critics are led by this new substantiality in the King's character to see a change in his function—one from God in Man to the voice of Man's benighted questionings.[28] The change (if it is that) is, however, neither incorrect nor inadvertent. Tennyson's precedent for this particular kind of divine despair is the anguished words from the cross, which Arthur's clearly recall: "My God, thou hast forgotten me in my death!" (l. 27). Involved here is a remote nod at the traditional idea of the Christian life as a reenactment of Christ's, but more immediately the allusion serves as a reminder that no degree of spirituality is exempt from the agonies of doubt.

Beset by forebodings before the "last weird battle in the west" and confirmed in his deepest dread after the struggle, with his knighthood shattered and himself "smitten thro' the helm," the King confesses his wintry thoughts to Sir Bedivere, "First made and latest left of all the knights": "O Bedivere, . . . on my heart hath fallen/Confusion, till I know not what I am,/Nor whence I am, nor whether I be king" (ll. 143–45).

Professor Baum regards it as disastrous, in view of Arthur's identification with "soul," that such confusion should come upon him at this point and make the close of the epic excessively pessimistic.[29] The King's uncertainty about his identity and origin, however, has a dramatic context; it is a temporary mood—quite distinct from the "doubt" that clouds his mind later in the poem, which refers simply to his sense of death's impenetrable mystery. Excalibur's mystical evanishment, the account of which Arthur at length hears as reassurance, to say nothing of his own words on the old order's changing, lead away from the King's mood of depression and bring the poem to its somber but by no means comfortless ending: Bedivere's watching Arthur's funeral barge "vanish into light" and the sunrise "bringing the new year."

Admittedly, there is an ambiguity in Arthur's admonition to Bedivere to "comfort thyself," and perhaps the idyll's most memorable feature is the evocation of the bereft Sir Bedivere, grieving for "the true old times" and contemplating his barren prospect:

> 'And I, the last, go forth companionless,
> And the days darken round me, and the years,
> Among new men, strange faces, other minds.
> (ll. 404–06)

Tennyson wrote these lines in the wake of his own grief for Arthur Hallam; their exactness and poignancy suggest that Tennyson's commitment to the consolatory view, though not "insincere" was, after all, theoretical and even a bit forced compared to his capacity for identifying with those who mourn.

Theoretical or not, however, the conclusion Arthur frames in response to Bedivere does resolve the tension that the whole course of the epic has insisted upon between the vulnerability of Arthur's kingdom and its value. Tennyson has presented, "parabolically," in the collapse of Arthur's Order the fate of all human absolutes in the face of inevitable change. The *Idylls of the King* is his rendering of the deep-rooted nineteenth-century drama of traditional values versus individual inclination, of moral absolutism versus relativism, of objective verities versus subjective impressions. In each of the forms this struggle took, Tennyson for his part sided with the forces of permanence and stability. Yet he was far from insensitive to the futility and pathos inherent in that choice. Arthur's sense that his cause does not wholly comprehend the social weal is an important element in his sorrow:

'Ill doom is mine
To war against my people and my knights.
The king who fights his people fights himself.
And they my knights, who loved me once, the stroke
That strikes them dead is as my death to me.'
(ll. 70–74)

His attempts to shore up his tottering authority may not only be destined to fail; they may also be, for that very reason, not wholly good. Hence must the old order change, yielding place to new—"Lest one good custom should corrupt the world." Arthur, in defeat, has won through to an affirmation contained in the work's culminating paradox: the unchanging is revealed through change, and "God fulfills himself in many ways."

Sir Harold Nicolson declared it a mystery to him that any judge of poetry could in these days admire the *Idylls of the King*.[30] Not many do; for, from the modern perspective, Tennyson's Arthuriad remains a strange, uncongenial work. Even when its relation to the tradition of heroic poetry is considered, as we have tried to consider it at the beginning of this discussion of the poem, it is difficult to take seriously a poetic romance—whatever its claims as epic—that was written in a period we associate with Balzac and Flaubert, Dickens and George Eliot, Tolstoy and Dostoevsky. The work of these great prose masters, and indeed the total nineteenth-century achievement in the novel, makes so different an attempt in narrative seem perhaps, at best, an act of poetic *hubris;* at worst, an unassimilable irrelevancy. Yet the more we ponder the difference of the *Idylls of the King* from what we regard as the mainstream of nineteenth-century narrative, the more this difference adds clarity and point to the kind of effort Tennyson's epic represents.

In following this critical tack, the place to begin is with that monumental precursor of the novel, Cervantes's *Don Quixote*. Its subject, like that of the *Idylls of the King*, is chivalry; but there, it goes without saying, the resemblance ends. Indeed, the two works approach that subject from nearly opposite directions. In *Don Quixote,* as the French critic René Girard has said, "chivalric existence is the imitation of Christ";[31] in the *Idylls* the imitation of Arthur by his knights, "Stamp'd with the image of the King" ("The Holy Grail," l. 24), representing the following of conscience, resembles the Christian's imitation of Christ. But, as Girard observes, "Cervantes' work is a long meditation on the baleful influence that the most lucid minds can exercise upon one another";[32] Tennyson's, on the other hand, traces out the baleful consequences of a breakdown in the "imitative" relationship.

Whatever way we read Cervantes's bafflingly elusive book, it satirizes social practice, whereas the *Idylls of the King* extols social ideals. Fielding, acknowledging his direct literary descent from Cervantes, saw as the very basis of his own comic art the exposure of affectation.[33] Flaubert's *Madame Bovary,* whose debt to *Don Quixote* is crucial, carries on this novelistic concern for the exposure of pretense and the substitution of realism for romance. "Bovaryism," as Jules de Gaultier defined it, is the attempt to see oneself as one is not by imitating the desires of another.[34] Tennyson, by contrast, upholds a positive view of emulation; for, in his poem, the "Other" incarnates one's best self (the knights "reverence the King, as if he were/Their conscience"). Flaubert turned upon his subject the cold eye of the dispassionate analyst; Tennyson sought in his own bardic voice to celebrate virtue and denounce vice: "How many among us at this very hour/Do forge a lifelong trouble for ourselves,/By taking true for false, or false for true . . . !" ("Geraint and Enid," ll. 2–4).

In England, a novel like Dickens's *Great Expectations,* with its jaundiced view of external, conventional standards of what constitutes a gentleman, shows even more pointedly how the novel typically opposes romance and tends to find in the ideals of society a source of illusion and self-deception. It is not, of course, that the *Idylls of the King* advocates self-deception—quite the contrary; but it does embody the "true" in an *ideal* of conduct in clear contrast to the novel's main work of analyzing the *realities* of human behavior.

As well as being a continuation of the tradition of the heroic poem, then, the *Idylls of the King* represents a reactionary alternative to the prevailing forms and purposes of narrative. Not by authorial intent but by virtue of its situation in the nineteenth-century literary milieu, the *Idylls* is—in a more relevant sense than the term is often used—an anti-novel.[35] As its name should remind us, the novel fulfills its function by bringing us the news—a function that has led Lionel Trilling to assign to the novel what he calls "a peculiar role as a *naturalizing* agent in culture. It has the effect," Trilling goes on to say, "of bringing into the circle of accepted things what at first seems strange, impossible, unacceptable."[36] In contrast to such a function, Tennyson's *Idylls* does not inform us about and accommodate us to the unfamiliar but champions the cause of conventionally accepted though embattled values. One way of putting it would be to conclude that the great nineteenth-century novelists, pursuing what Mr. Trilling calls in another place the novel's "perpetual quest for reality,"[37] were following the lead of Cervantes; Tennyson, on the other hand, taking chivalry seriously by making it stand for the old verities that give order and coherence to the moral life, was being essentially quixotic. The term suggests the measure of his epic's right to our disparagement and praise.

CHAPTER 4

The Dramatic Poet

IN HIS early years Tennyson was ready enough to use poetry as outright self-expression, but what he expressed was often more a conventional attitude than an original and intensely personal feeling. Still in his teens, he had recorded in print "the gloom of mis-spent years" and his wanderings "in darkness and sorrow,/Unfriended, and cold, and alone." Soon after, he was unwarily committing to verse ecstatic gushings over a "darling room" and sour invective against "crusty," "rusty," "musty," "fusty" Christopher North. Of course the personal note not only persists in his later work but broadens and deepens to *In Memoriam*, remaining to the last in such poems as "Merlin and the Gleam" and "Crossing the Bar."

But even so, there is no mistaking the change from youthful, even brash, effusiveness to a canny reserve that reveals itself at the end of the "ten years' silence" in 1842. One of the crucial signs, or better, consequences of this change is Tennyson's recurrent assumption of a voice or *persona* distinct from himself in poems more or less classifiable as dramatic monologues. From the volumes of 1842, where the monologue emerges distinctively with "Ulysses," "Saint Simeon Stylites," and "Locksley Hall," until the end of his career, it continues to be a major Tennysonian form.

Even Tennyson's lyrics—or, at least, the most memorable ones—bear witness to a divided mind; and in monologues he could encompass, not necessarily more effectively but perhaps more readily, more comfortably, his disparate and conflicting attitudes. On the one hand, an essentially "dialogic" confrontation may be internalized and intensified by soliloquy. On the other, the oppositions may be represented through ironic tensions between the speaker and his dramatic situation or between his perspective and that of his implied audience. What can result in either case is that a report upon experience, which if made by other means would seem contradictory or merely inconclusive, becomes resonant and comprehensive.

An assembly of Tennyson's monologues reveals several rather distinct categories. One group, the most difficult to label, might be called "confessional monologues." Another, a variety of domestic idyll, we shall designate as "pathetic monologues." From these must be distinguished their country cousins, Tennyson's dialect poems. "Historical monologues" and "mythological monologues" (the latter often referred to as "classical idylls") make up the last two classifications. These groupings are not absolute, but they do reflect important differences. To consider each category in turn reveals the range of purposes and effects that Tennyson sought to achieve in this form, and it also serves as one means of sorting out his more successful dramatic monologues from those that are inferior or of little consequence.

I *Confessional Monologues*

The term "confessional monologue" refers to a kind of poem in which the speaker is less a dramatic character than an objectification of certain qualities or aspects of what could be called the "lyrical *I*." If, in pure lyric, the poet is, for the moment, wholly absorbed in the lyrical voice of his poem and if, in pure drama, he is wholly detached from his characters, Tennyson's dissociation from the speaker is incomplete but crucial in these confessional monologues. It is not a question of the poet's having inadvertently attributed his own outlook to a dramatic character, and in a sense it is precisely the reverse of making a character the author's spokesman; Tennyson's *personae* serve not so much to transmit his views as to assume, and thereby try, his sentiments.

What distinguishes these confessional monologue poems, then, is the way in which the author's identity with his *persona* is at once asserted and withheld. It is a continuation in dramatic terms of the ambivalence revealed in the antithetical pair of lyrics "Nothing Will Die" and "All Things Will Die" (1830) and in that debate within "a divided will," "The Two Voices" (1842). "Supposed Confessions of a Second-rate Sensitive Mind" (1830) marks a rudimentary attempt to encompass these ambivalences dramatically. Were it not for the title, however, this piece could stand only as the poet's indulgence in a fit of personal melancholy; but, by the rather disingenuous means of crediting its sentiments to this vaguely specified source, Tennyson detaches himself from them. Within the poem itself, there is no irony present to effect such a separation; and the title alone is not enough to transform a sophomoric lyric poem into an effective dramatic one.

In "Locksley Hall" (1842), the dark mood of the speaker is less morbid and more adequately motivated. A degree of genuine dramatic objectivity is attained, not by disowning the emotions of the *persona* as in the "Supposed Confessions," but by endowing the speaker with a more distinct and separate identity. His sense of deprivation and embittered longing is essentially that of the young Tennyson himself, but it is given solid grounding in the particular context of a dramatic situation. As a result, the familiar emotional contours of much of the early poetry take on greater depth and perspective in "Locksley Hall."

The protagonist's situation and outlook are epitomized in his relationship to the hall itself. As the scene of his reverie, Locksley Hall becomes by the end of the poem a veritable symbol of the past. The unfaithfulness of his cousin Amy, however, has dissolved this idyllic past and left the Hamletesque hero stranded on the sterile promontory of the present:

> O my cousin shallow-hearted! O my Amy, mine no more!
> O the dreary, dreary moorland! O the barren barren shore!

Paraphrasing Dante (*Inferno*, V, 121–23), he asserts "That a sorrow's crown of sorrow is remembering happier things"; thus a nostalgic reverie, begun in an effort to abate the emptiness of the present, only makes it less tolerable. Therefore, the speaker turns his thoughts from the past to the future, invoking the *Zeitgeist* ("Mother-Age") to restore his former zealous faith in human progress:

> Can I but relive in sadness? I will turn that earlier page.
> Hide me from my deep emotion, O thou wondrous Mother-Age!
>
> Make me feel the wild pulsations that I felt before the strife,
> When I heard my days before me, and the tumult of my life.

But to "mix with action" will not redeem the protagonist's personal loss; whatever the "march of mind" might bring with it, he will reap no "harvest of his youthful joys." As recollection has done, anticipation of the future merely intensifies his sense of isolation, as "the individual withers, and the world is more and more."

Having failed to dispel his melancholy by contemplating the past and future, Tennyson's hero is drawn next toward not a temporal but a spatial escape—to "some retreat/Deep in yonder shining Orient." But, for all its appeal, the primitive existence is no valid alternative for this product of his time and place, "heir of all the ages, in the foremost files of time." He rejects it; and, with a melodramatic cry of "Forward, forward," he places himself once again in the van of progress. Such a prospect, with such solace as it can give, fittingly culminates in the hero's acceptance of the inevitable doom of Locksley Hall itself:

> Howsoever these things be, a long farewell to Locksley Hall!
> Now for me the woods may wither, now for me the roof-tree fall.
> . . . .
> Let it fall on Locksley Hall, with rain or hail, or fire or snow;
> For the mighty wind arises, roaring seaward, and I go.

Having thus freed himself from the ancestral home and the past it represents, the protagonist can rejoin his comrades, not rejuvenated but presumably able to reclaim his social nature and brave the winds of change.

In the sequel, "Locksley Hall Sixty Years After" (1886), the same speaker, weighed down by years and full of dismay at the changes they have brought, lectures his grandson, who has been jilted for an older, richer man and who has also been blighted by modern unbelief. Surveying the scene to which the times have brought him, Tennyson's aged hero sees little that has come to good. The marvels of his youth have shrunk to commonplaces; the ideal of democracy has degenerated into a dreary leveling and a chaotic inversion of values; art itself wallows in the foul troughs of Zolaist Naturalism. His assessment is typical of the splenetic elder: "When was age so cramm'd with menace? madness? written, spoken lies?"

Overwrought as the hero of the first "Locksley Hall" may be, he nevertheless cuts a compelling figure compared to the hero of the second with his selfish contempt for his grandson's feelings and in his sweeping condemnation of the rising generation. Read as a series of pronouncements, "Locksley Hall Sixty Years After" is an intensely unattractive poem; it fares much better, however, when read as "drama." The point is not that the aged hero's comments do not reflect Tennyson's own dissatisfactions in his later years—in large measure, they do—but that the poem represents the speaker's undergoing a drastic change in attitude; he is rising above his discontent rather than running it into the ground. His very denunciations modulate from mere reactionary outrage to humane indignation, and his almost total self-absorption gives way to a measure of self-awareness. The old man seeks his grandson's pardon and recognizes the partiality of his own judgment:

Nay, you pardon, cry your 'Forward,' yours are hope and youth, but I—
Eighty winters leave the dog too lame to follow with the cry,

Lame and old and past his time, and passing now into the night;
Yet I would the rising race were half as eager for the light.

Self-pity is not wholly absent from these lines, but the gain in objectivity should nevertheless be marked.

And, though he expresses many objectionable sentiments in the process, Tennyson's hero does talk himself around to generous-heartedness in the end. That dramatic unfolding, rather than the sum of its observations on the quality of modern life, is the larger concern of the poem. The speaker finally can do justice to the man now dead whom he wronged, affirming love—not "the sounding watch-word, 'Evolution' "—to be the true transforming power: "Forward, let the stormy moment fly and mingle with the past./I that loathed have come to love him. Love will conquer at the last."

"The Ancient Sage" (1885), another poem of Tennyson's old age, presents a much more static character and one more fully identifiable with the author. Tennyson, in fact, insisted on the poem's closeness to his own personal feelings.[1] What dramatic quality it has comes from the interplay between the sage's own words and the verses from a scroll that an aspiring poet has put in his hands. The result is not so much an internal debate in "The Two Voices" manner as an antiphony between the young man's skeptical song and the seer's resolute affirmations of a "Faith beyond the forms of Faith." The dialogue of the mind with itself has dwindled here into an unfair contest, with the voice of doubt and intellectual protest safely hedged about by the sage's impenetrable assurance. Naturally the sage has the last word, but the only ones that are really memorable are those in which he recalls his "Passion of the Past."

II *Pathetic Monologues*

To label a second type of dramatic poem "pathetic monologues" is perhaps to hint at why these pieces—over a dozen throughout the span of Tennyson's work—do not require extended commentary. They aim at nothing beyond the evoking of tender feeling; and, in pursuing this objective, they sometimes descend to unpardonable depths of sentimentality. Where the speakers in the "confessional monologues" tend to be only partially distinguishable from the author himself, the speakers in these poems could by no means be mistaken for the poet in disguise. For all that, they are at best sketchily characterized; the protagonist of one pathetic monologue speaks with much the same voice heard in others. It is the narrative element that actually dominates in most monologues of this kind. The story is told by the protagonist only as a means of heightening the pathos. In nearly every instance the narrator/actor is a woman: abandoned sweetheart, grieving mother, dutiful or conscience-stricken wife.

Tennyson's sources for these poems were usually tales told to him by friends or ones retailed by popular journalism. By setting them to verse, he could seldom add substance to or make more enduring the superficial appeal that caught his undernourished fancy in the first place. Nor is the verse itself much more than doggerel, the commonest form being rhymed couplets in irregular meter with six stresses to the line, or—as in this not unfair illustration of their sodden worst from "The Flight"—seven: "Speak to me, sister, counsel me; this marriage must not be./You only know the love that makes the world a world to me!"

As for their narrative substance, a few examples indicate the sort of fare they offer. In "The First Quarrel" a remorseful widow tells her doctor how learning of her husband's premarital liaison led her to quarrel with him on the eve of a journey on which he was drowned. "In the Children's Hospital" is a pious, selfless nurse's account of how a little girl facing surgery overhears a doctor despair of her chances and dies peacefully before she can be subjected to the callous surgeon's knife. "Happy" or "The Leper's Bride" goes back to the Middle Ages for its scene in which a wife demonstrates her faithfulness to the wedding vow by joining her husband in his living death: "A little nearer? Yes. I shall hardly be content/Till I be leper like yourself, my love, from head to heel."

One exception exists among this dismal lot: in "Rizpah," Tennyson brings the pathetic monologue somewhere near the condition of art. For once, in the figure of the deranged and dying mother, Tennyson has created a distinctive speaker; and she, rather than the tale she tells, provides the center of interest. However, the story of her son's being hanged in chains for robbing the mail and of her having collected and buried his bones as they fell from the gibbet unfolds with a timing that yields the fullest measure of shock and sympathy. Moreover, the auditor, a lady in charitable attendance at the old woman's deathbed, is "present" to a degree unusual in these pathetic monologues; and her presence is made to count, for the contrast between the roles in which fate has cast the two women adds an effective poignancy:

> Ah—you, that have lived so soft, what should *you* know of the night,
> The blast and the burning shame and the bitter frost and the fright?
> I have done it, while you were asleep—you were only made for the day.
> I have gather'd my baby together—and now you may go your way.

Even the lurching hexameter couplets seem in this instance an appropriate vehicle for the speaker's emotions. Her derangement acts not as a distraction from but as an intensification of a mother's most human grief. In its fierceness, her maternal love stands out stark and convincing, as stripped to the bare bones as the body of her son.

III *Monologues in Dialect*

In some ways Tennyson's monologues in dialect resemble pathetic monologues—they deal with the concerns of plain people and carry the homely manner to its farthest extreme—but they deserve the distinction of a separate category on at least two important counts. For one thing, they are not essentially pathetic narrations but character vignettes in which the flavor of living speech is the distinguishing quality. For another, they possess something none of Tennyson's other monologues can claim: a sense of what Stopford Brooke has described with a certain excess of solemnity as "that elemental humorousness of things."[2]

The best known and most successful of Tennyson's dialect poems are "Northern Farmer, Old Style" (1864) and "Northern Farmer, New Style" (1870). Like all the others—except one—they are written in the Lincolnshire dialect familiar to Tennyson from his boyhood at Somersby. The first is a death-bed scene, but there is nothing lugubrious about it. All that weighs heavily on the old style farmer's mind, besides the fact that his doctor has denied him his usual pint of ale, is the Almighty's dubious justice in taking a man so busy with his fields and stock when there is no lack of idlers He might have called to Himself. With equanimity, he admits his probable paternity of "Bessy Marris's barne"—it being altogether likely, "for she wur a bad un, sheä." Tennyson caps this comic irony at the conclusion when the farmer orders his nurse to bring the ale, staunchly insisting with mock heroism that his daily pint is a rule he means to uphold to the death: "I weänt breäk rules fur Doctor, a knaws naw moor nor a floy;/Git ma my ääle, I tell tha, an' if I mun doy I mun doy." Tennyson's picture of the new style farmer in the companion piece is less sympathetic, though the farmer's outspoken materialism invites laughter more than high-minded condemnation. As he rides along with his son, the very sound of his horse's hoofs proclaiming the ultimate virtue of "proputty, proputty, proputty," he berates the boy for wanting to marry for love rather than land.

None of the half-dozen other excursions in dialect measures up to the "Northern Farmers," though each has a charm of its own to repay the struggle with the oddities of Tennyson's phonetic spelling. "Will Waterproof's Lyrical Monologue" (1842), a memorial to a famous London tavern and the solace of which Tennyson was wont to partake there during part of the "ten years' silence," is not one of the dialect poems, though it bears them some family resemblance. Considering it in the list, however, makes apparent what Tennyson gained by moving from the conversational to the dialectal. The difference between "Will Waterproof" and the best dialect pieces is the difference between wit, which Tennyson could never sustain with real grace, and broad humor. In the poems of such humor the coarse side of his nature becomes an asset rather than a hidden liability. We should not make extravagant claims for these monologues, but it would be a pity to neglect their refreshing testimony to Tennyson's willingness to come down from yonder mountain height of Victorian earnestness.

IV *Historical Monologues*

Tennyson's historical monologues have little but the historicity of their speakers in common, save that by coincidence nearly all of them touch directly or obliquely on religious matters. But however miscellaneous these monologues by historical characters may be as a group, they include two of Tennyson's most successful poems in the dramatic mode. The first of these is "Saint Simeon Stylites," one of his earliest dramatic monologues and one of the few that stand comparison—in terms of the relative excellence of similar qualities—with the best of Robert Browning's. Simeon's dilations upon his contemptibility and saintliness present a curious but convincing juxtaposition of self-abasement and pride. Tennyson manages to combine these seemingly contradictory qualities as the hemispheres of an all-encompassing fanaticism. He makes quite credible Simeon's insistence upon his vileness as the basis of his claim to sainthood:

> I, Simeon of the pillar
> . . . .
> do now
> From my high nest of penance here proclaim
> That Pontius and Iscariot by my side
> Show'd like fair seraphs.
> . . . .
> God only thro' his bounty hath thought fit,
> Among the powers and princes of this world,
> To make me an example to mankind,
> Which few can reach to.

Tennyson is not giving us here another Tartuffe; Saint Simeon atop his pillar, clutching his sufferings to himself as the fee he hopes will buy him heaven, is something quite other than the conventional pious fraud. He is religious asceticism, which Tennyson would regard tragically in "The Holy Grail," tuned to the pitch of comic absurdity.

"Boädicéa" (1864), representing the barbaric yawp of a British queen inciting her people against the Romans, is a metrical experiment on a model from Catullus.[3] All the other historical monologues, as well as those on mythological subjects (to be discussed presently), are written in blank verse. "Sir John Oldcastle, Lord Cobham" (1880), the reflections of a fugitive from religious tyranny, and "Columbus" (1880), written, the poet's son tells us, "after repeated entreaties from certain prominent Americans that he would commemorate the discovery of America in verse,"[4] are easily forgotten memorials to men of courage, though Columbus's readiness "to sail forth on one last voyage" gives that poem some interest as a thematic extension of "Ulysses." The subject of "Romney's Remorse" (1889) is the eighteenth-century painter who forsook his wife, acting upon Reynolds's notion that marriage was the ruination of the artist, but was nursed by her in his last days. The poem reflects some of the suspicion of Art with a capital "A" that must have been deeply engrained in Tennyson, and the painter's discontent with his artistic achievement may also be a personal note.

The dreams of the Mogul Emperor in "Akbar's Dream" (1892) are the tranquil vision of a Truth and a Power that lie behind the contending forms of faith and the reassuring one that even the dismantling of an old order is but the prelude to the rearing of a more lofty edifice. Those of the Roman poet-philosopher in the fine "Lucretius" (1868) are the vexed nightmares of a spirit torn between the promptings of passion and thought. As Tennyson relates in the explanatory introduction to the monologue proper, Lucretius has been given a philter by his wife Lucilla in the hope that his passion for her will be rekindled. The drug, however, has "Confused the chemic labor of the blood," leaving him wracked by hallucinations whose memory disturbs even his rational intervals. Yet it is misleading to call the poem, as one of Tennyson's most valuable critics has done, "a study in abnormal psychology . . . a study in morbid degeneration."[5] Lucretius is finally more the victim of his intellectual position than of his wife's destructive potion.

What the potion has done is to dramatize within the character Lucretius the struggle between Sense and Conscience that Tennyson had allegorized as a very young poet and made a dominant theme of his Arthurian epic. Lucretian philosophy, with its rational self-sufficiency and its exaltation of "the sober majesties/Of settled, sweet, Epicurean life," cannot cope with the revelations into human nature that his evil dreams have brought him. For the naturalistic basis of his philosophy leaves him with no hopes beyond the physical existence which he now sees as inescapably bestial:

> . . . it seems some unseen monster lays
> His vast and filthy hands upon my will,
> Wrenching it backward into his, and spoils
> My bliss in being.

It is calm, the "sacred everlasting calm" exemplified by "the Gods who haunt/The lucid interspace of world and world," for which Lucretius in his anguish thirsts. The very calm of nature, succeeding a night of storm, mocks his troubled state; but it also prefigures death itself, the tranquil close to life's storms. That alternative, at least, Lucretius is free enough to choose. But the choice is not exempt from irony; his longing for death's "divine Tranquility" closes in a most violent scene: "With that he drove the knife into his side./She heard him raging, heard him fall, ran in,/Beat breast, tore hair. . . ."

This poem touches many concerns over which in other poems Tennyson is given to moralizing—in particular, the dire consequences of materialism. In "Lucretius," however, these concerns do not keep Tennyson from his primary responsibility, as poet, of imagining his way into the character and his particular situation. Classicists are in almost unanimous agreement that the distillation of the Lucretian essence is masterful. Even more to the point, the Lucretian spirit has been made flesh, with the result that the poem has not merely the accuracy of an intellectual paradigm but the wholeness of a dramatic recreation.

V *Mythological Monologues*

Tennyson's mythological monologues consist mainly of his five major poems on Greek subjects, often referred to as "classical idylls." However, room must also be made here for reference to a work of a quite different sort: "The Voyage of Maeldune" (1880), a first-person narrative based on a tale in P. W. Joyce's *Old Celtic Romances*. The poem recounts a symbolic voyage by the hero and his comrades, who seek vengeance upon the slayer of Maeldune's father. At each of several islands, representing various excesses encountered on life's journey, the mariners are goaded on by misadventure or their own discontent. Coming at last to the Isle of a Saint, Maeldune is urged to surrender his bloody purpose and heed the Lord's admonition that "Vengeance is mine!" Thus, weary with travel, Maeldune sails within sight of his father's slayer but leaves him in peace and makes for his homeland. In Tennyson's telling, the tale does not quite embody, as one authority claims, "the futility of recrimination and the necessity of love," [6] since merely ignoring one's enemy is hardly the same as loving him. As allegory, the poem is, in fact, rather thin and obvious; its appeal lies mainly in the vivid presentation of its incidents in a plain and vigorous style.

An allegorical intention is also present in Tennyson's earliest classical idyll, "Oenone" (1833, much revised 1842). In Oenone's recital of the judgment of Paris is framed the parable of human choice among power (Heré), wisdom (Pallas), and beauty (Aphrodite). The strong element of narrative and the particular qualities of both the tale and its teller also link the poem to Tennyson's pathetic monologues. In later mythological monologues Tennyson came to treat the "story" more implicitly, as inferentially "given" in the mythical subject; and this handling allowed him to concentrate more on individualizing the speaker than he can in "Oenone." Yet it is nearly as true of the other mythological monologues as it is of "Oenone" that what Tennyson aims at is not the kind of particularized characterization that we expect of the monologue, if we conceive the form in terms of such acknowledged triumphs of their kind as Browning's "My Last Duchess" or "The Bishop Orders His Tomb." In commenting upon Tennyson's 1842 volumes, one contemporary critic found that "His characters, with few exceptions, are generalizations, or refined abstractions, clearly developing certain thoughts, feelings, and forms." [7] This assessment applies with especial aptness to Tennyson's mythological figures; they are the idealized incarnation of *moods* rather than realistically portrayed personages. To say so is not to disparage these poems but to essay some definition of their artistic effect —the effect of an essentially lyric feeling both objectified by the dramatic form and universalized by the mythic subject.

In "Oenone," however, the various elements of the poem are not perfectly wedded. The moral allegory and the lament of an abandoned nymph seem essentially unrelated. No doubt Tennyson assumed that, since Oenone's grief is a result of Paris's rejection of wisdom in favor of beauty, there is relation enough between the emotions and the message. But merely in terms of the allegorical meaning of Paris's fateful judgment, Oenone's abandonment—pathetic as that may be—is not the essential consequence of his choice. Much more significant is the destruction of Troy, and Tennyson himself acknowledges as much when he concludes the poem with his heroine's vague premonition of the burning city. Yet the adumbration of Troy's flames in Oenone's searing jealousy counts little toward making the emotional texture of the monologue appropriate to the allegory and its promotion of "self-reverence, self-knowledge, self-control." Perhaps that is why the moral content of the poem seems so obtrusive—why Pallas's speech reminds us (had we the fine fancy of Douglas Bush) of Queen Victoria addressing the Duke of Argyll.[8]

At its best the poem is, in fact, above everything else a virtuoso exercise in word painting. Its description of the vale of Ida and the decorative tableaux of the goddesses lull the senses rather than arouse the sympathies or quicken moral awareness. Whatever reservations must persist about the poem as a total conception, it contains passages of extraordinary loveliness.

Incongruity of a somewhat similar kind also poses a problem in that quite different work, "Ulysses" (1842). An old man's indomitable resolution, not a young girl's sorrow, is the burden of the song; but it too is a song whose sound and sense do not quite merge. W. W. Robson, in one of the many excellent contributions to the interpretive controversy that has built up around this famous poem, states the case thus: "Tennyson, the responsible social being, the admirably serious and 'committed' Victorian intellectual, is uttering strenuous sentiments in the accent of Tennyson the most un-strenuous, lonely, and poignant of poets." [9]

Tennyson is on record that "Ulysses . . . gave my feeling about the need of going forward, and braving the struggle of life," [10] and this personal feeling broadens into a kind of challenge to his times in Ulysses' concluding reference to the "will/To strive, to seek, to find, and not to yield." On the other hand, the "newer world" he seeks is conceived in terms of a lotos-land tranquility with the ultimate goal an eternal rest: "To sail beyond the sunset, and the baths/Of all the western stars, until I die." Thus it would appcar that Tennyson's hero is "braving the struggle of life" by attempting to escape it.

Involved in the poem's contradictions are not only the conflicts between Tennyson's "two voices" but also the rich complexity of his hero's literary ancestry. Tennyson looks back to Homer's keen and resourceful Odysseus, but more vividly before him is the *Ulisse* of Dante's *Inferno*. The situation of Ulysses' resuming his travels comes from Canto XXVI, and the many echoes of that passage make it hard to suppose that Dante's having placed Ulysses among the evil counselors can be wholly irrelevant to Tennyson's characterization. Goethe's Faust and the melodramatic heroes of Byron may also figure in the genealogy.[11]

Consequently, no simple, unambiguous interpretation of Tennyson's monologue can assimilate its many nuances. To begin with, we have to confront the implications of a man well past his prime who is setting forth upon an adventure as if his life were before him. The image of "this gray spirit yearning in desire/To follow knowledge like a sinking star" may be noble, but is it not sadder—even more sadly ironic—than nobility ought to be? Then there is the contrast between Ulysses and his son Telemachus, which at least pointedly reverses the conventional relationship. It is the father whom we see restless and eager to leave the nest, whereas the son typifies "slow prudence" and dedication to "common duties." Later, in the voice of King Arthur, Tennyson would condemn such abdication of irksome responsibilities:

> '. . . the King must guard
> That which he rules, and is but as the hind
> To whom a space of land is given to plow,
> Who may not wander from the allotted field
> Before his work be done.'
> ("The Holy Grail," ll. 901–905)

What, finally, are we to think of an elderly veteran who complains of being "matched with an aged wife" and for whom the crown of heroic adventure consists of a reunion with his comrade-in-arms—"It may be we shall touch the Happy Isles,/And see the great Achilles, whom we knew"?

But it would be a perverse reading that allowed such questions to obscure Tennyson's fundamental sympathy with his hero. In Ulysses' sense of alienation from his surroundings, we encounter a familiar Tennysonian motif. Likewise, it is typical that his vision of the future should involve the appeasement of nostalgia. That same desire to escape the wearisome present Tennyson recognized in himself, just as he expresses it through his hero; but it is after all the counter-melody to the main theme—a negative emotion which an affirmative must transcend. Thus the mood of "Ulysses" is resolute though rooted in a sense of weakness as well as strength. Unlike the exultant self-confidence of "Sir Galahad" ("My strength is as the strength of ten,/Because my heart is pure"), Ulysses expresses a humility befitting the inherent irony of his situation: "that which we are, we are,—/One equal temper of heroic hearts,/Made weak by time and fate." Tennyson achieves a moving characterization in "Ulysses"—as he does not in "Sir Galahad"—because the heroic quality does not conceal the normal human frailties which call it forth and with which it is inseparably allied.

Kindred to his protagonist's weakness, just as he is admiring of his strength, Tennyson could make of Ulysses perhaps his most truly appropriate version of the Victorian hero. "I am a part of all that I have met," Ulysses affirms out of an awareness of his place in the unfolding panorama of human experience and achievement. Such awareness brings with it a determination to forge still farther along the path of progress: "To follow knowledge like a sinking star,/Beyond the utmost bound of human thought"—a Victorian ideal par excellence.

More disconcerting, however—and perhaps more revealing of a Victorian Ulysses—is his fear that the current age may not be equal to the demands of the future ("We are not now that strength which in old days/Moved earth and heaven"), or that past achievements have exacted a price of spiritual exhaustion that has placed new attainments beyond reach. He and his men have been "Made weak by time and fate," and Ulysses seems to foresee that disaster Dante had described for him: "It may be that the gulfs will wash us down." The tone is precisely that of another great Victorian, Matthew Arnold, for whom the relevant heroic stance was similarly neither to deny whatever was inauspicious at the present time nor to allow it to deter the courageous intelligence from persevering. "That promised land," Arnold wrote in reference to a new cultural epoch, "it will not be ours to enter, and we shall die in the wilderness: but to have desired to enter it, to have saluted it from afar, is already, perhaps, the best distinction among contemporaries." [12]

The traditional account of "Tithonus," which was conceived as a companion piece to "Ulysses," but not finished until 1859, is that it was inspired by a remark of the poet's sister Emily—sorrowing for Arthur Hallam, to whom she was betrothed—to the effect that "the Tennysons never die." [13] At any rate, it is customary to see in Tennyson's handling of the myth of a mortal to whom the goddess of the dawn out of love granted immortality but not the accompanying gift of eternal youth "the embodiment of his own sense of life's intolerable burden." [14] Yet too great an emphasis on the poem's relation to Tennyson's personal dejection and the grief that surrounded him in the wake of Hallam's death leads to some distortions of its meaning. It is a useful corrective to take very seriously the fact that "Tithonus" and "Ulysses" belong together, not only in their bearing upon Tennyson's private tragedy, but as an antithetical pair of imaginary portraits.

The two poems—and this is not to deny the "autobiographical" element—are mutually illuminating as a formal exercise in the contrast of elemental human types, somewhat as are Milton's "L'Allegro" and "Il Penseroso." Ulysses' is the voice of avidity for living:

> How dull it is to pause, to make an end,
> To rust unburnish'd, not to shine in use!
> As tho' to breathe were life! Life piled on life
> Were all too little. . . .

Tithonus's is the voice of satiety:

> Why should a man desire in any way
> To vary from the kindly race of men,
> Or pass beyond the goal of ordinance
> Where all should pause, as is most meet for all?

Together they strike a note in harmony with Oscar Wilde's famous *mot* that one of life's tragedies is wanting what we cannot have; the other is getting it.

Tithonus's primary longing is not for the release of death but for the recovery of his humanity; the curse is not life but that he must live alienated, as neither god nor mortal. When we look at the poem in this way, "Tithonus" seems less the product of Tennyson's grief than of his reflections upon the fate of the artist.[15] The situation of Tithonus—his love for Eos and her gift of a kind of immortal mortality—figures forth the condition of the poet and the consequences of his devotion to the beautiful. Eos, the goddess of the dawn, is clearly associated with the source of imaginative power and her love for Tithonus with poetic inspiration, for the sounds she whispers in his ear are likened to those by which the god of poetry himself built the walls of Troy (ll. 61–63). Tithonus's peculiar immortality suggests those powers by which his devotion to the esthetic ideal distinguishes the artist.

In his hero Tennyson illustrates the ambiguous nature of those artistic gifts. The poet's power to envision eternal beauty, rather than freeing him from the clog of mortal imperfection, actually intensifies his consciousness of it; for he is condemned "To dwell in presence of immortal youth,/Immortal age beside immortal youth." More painful still is the realization that his aspirations and special gifts have isolated the poet from the sphere of human sympathy—"from the kindly race of men. . . . the homes/Of happy men." Like the realm of the artist, then, the portals of the dawn guard a limbo where the ideal is beheld but never fully attained, where mortal weakness remains without mortal consolation, and where divine aspiration leads to "Godlike isolation."[16] The "gleaming halls of morn" that Tithonus roams as a white-haired shadow bear less similarity to a conventional house of mourning than to the typically Tennysonian palace of art.

Though neither especially penetrating nor original commentary, a final word on "Tithonus" must be one that acknowledges it as a singularly beautiful poem. Its opening lines exhibit a control of movement and melody that hardly slackens to the very end:

> The woods decay, the woods decay and fall,
> The vapours weep their burthen to the ground,
> Man comes and tills the field and lies beneath,

And after many a summer dies the swan.
Me only cruel immortality
Consumes; I wither slowly in thine arms,
Here at the quiet limit of the world. . . .

There are other, more solid kinds of beauty; but this type is the sort Tennyson wrought to perfection. "Tithonus" could have been written by no other poet.

In "Tiresias" (published in 1885 but partly written much earlier), Tennyson returns to the theme of the poet's estrangement from society. His version of Tiresias's tragic situation is borrowed from Callimachus, undoubtedly as being suited to the parallel he wished to exploit between the ancient prophet and the modern poet. Accordingly, unlike T. S. Eliot's "Old man with wrinkled female breasts," Tennyson's Tiresias has not throbbed between two lives but has gazed upon the naked Pallas, who takes away his sight and curses him with the fatal gift of prophecy: "Henceforth be blind, for thou hast seen too much,/And speak the truth that no man may believe."

As in "Tithonus," Tennyson expresses his sense of the ambiguous consequences of the poetic vision, but he does so more self-righteously. The poet-sage's glimpse at "Ineffable beauty" and his prophetic powers isolate him from the world, and his wisdom is scorned when most needed:

To cast wise words among the multitude
Was flinging fruit to lions; nor, in hours
Of civil outbreak, when I knew the twain
Would each waste each, and bring on both the yoke
Of stronger states, was mine the voice to curb
The madness of our cities and their kings.

Thus the poet's meed is neglect and a feeling of frustration and uselessness. Though Tennyson could hardly have complained of neglect in his later years, he did share Tiresias's sense that "This power hath worked no good to aught that lives,/And these blind hands were useless in their wars." "I tried in my 'Idylls' to teach men . . . the need of the Ideal," Tennyson is reported to have told his son. "But I feel sometimes as if my life had been a very useless life." [17]

In urging Menœceus to seek martyrdom, Tiresias echoes that insistence upon noble action as the height of virtue so recurrent in Tennyson's work: "the sun, the moon, the stars/Send no such light upon the ways of men/As one great deed." But these words, which send Menœceus to his death for the sake of Thebes, are spoken by one wholly removed from and unsuited to the life of action. Tiresias's melancholy is deepened by his consciousness of the contrast between Menœceus's heroic fate and his own: "Fairer thy fate than mine, if life's best end/Be to end well!" The prophet foresees that the young man "will achieve his greatness"; for himself there is only the welcome end of a life little prized: "But for me,/I would that I were gather'd to my rest,/And mingled with the famous kings of old."

In an epilogue to "Tiresias," Tennyson's enduring concern with the question of immortality leads him to contrast Tiresias's melancholy view of life and his pagan's circumscribed view of death with the peaceful passing of his lifelong friend Edward FitzGerald and the Christian promise it calls to mind. In the last of his mythological monologues, "Demeter and Persephone" (1889), Tennyson again takes up the theme of immortality and, in a more accomplished poem, is able to comprehend it wholly within his treatment of the mythical subject itself.

"Oenone," Tennyson's earliest monologue on a Classical subject, fails to fuse the imagery, the dominant feeling portrayed in the speaker, and the poem's ethical or philosophic content. In "Demeter and Persephone" the interconnection of these same three elements forms the poem's chief structural pattern and constitutes its particular success.[18] The myth's seasonal aspects provide the poem with its dominant imagery. Demeter's desolation is portrayed against a winter landscape; her joyful reunion with Persephone is accompanied by sun and flowers. The thematic opposition of life and death is also conveyed through varied references to day/night and spring/winter contrasts. Thus, the "nature myth" elements do not burden the poem as nonessential detail but provide the integral metaphoric means by which emotion is portrayed and the theme of immortality is delineated.

Hallam Tennyson recalls that "Demeter and Persephone" "was written at my request, because I knew that he [Tennyson] considered Demeter one of the most beautiful types of motherhood." [19] If we must mark this as Victorian sentimentalism, at least the sentimental view of the myth had the support of the prevailing scholarly one. One contemporary comparative mythologist described the Homeric hymn to Demeter as "an exquisite picture of the mourning mother and her beautiful child." [20] The poem itself does, in fact, escape the really damaging effects of sentiment in its emotional portraiture of maternal bereavement and love; for, unlike the mawkish treatment such matters receive in several of the pathetic monologues, the characters and situation do in this case possess the austerity and dignity of mythic types.

Thematically, as well as imagistically, "Demeter and Persephone" finds its center in the relationship between opposites. The numerous allusions to spring and winter, day and night, light and dark all point toward the crucial duality of life and death. However, the poem is not concerned simply with opposition but with relationship—with the fact that life and death derive their meanings from each other. Thus Demeter's reaction to the loss of her daughter is the inevitable realization that in the midst of life we are in death. The flowery fields of Enna are scarred by the chasm through which Persephone was drawn to Hades; Demeter is reminded that "The Bright one in the highest/Is brother of the Dark one in the lowest"; and this involvement of death in life is similarly suggested by Persephone herself as daughter of the Earth Mother and bride of Death.

Yet in the development of the poem these details become susceptible of an inverse interpretation: not death in life, but life in death. Earth's scar is healed: "all the space/Of blank earth-baldness clothes itself afresh"; Zeus, the brother of the Darkness, decrees that Persephone spend three-quarters of the year with Demeter; and the bonds of death yield to the power of maternal love. Nor is that all, for Tennyson's vision attempts to encompass not only the reconcilement of life to death but even the attainment of ultimate triumph, "Till thy dark lord accept and love the Sun,/And all the Shadow die into the Light."

This statment may be taken as the anticipation, from the speaker's pagan perspective, of the Christian dispensation; in any case, it expresses, in his particular accents of evolutionism, Tennyson's own dim yet emotion-tinged faith in that "one far-off divine event/To which the whole creation moves."

Although Tennyson's poem grounds the myth of Demeter and Persephone in the phenomena of nature, human feelings, and religio-philosophical conceptions, the monologue is a unified construct and not a series of heterogeneous layers. Just as both the theme of immortality and the "human" situation are conveyed through the details of the nature myth, so the theme rises out of the portrayal of emotion. The dominant emotion is love, afflicted with grief yet transcending it; and love, in a number of ways, lies at the heart of those intimations of immortality that the poem glimpses. It is, first of all, Demeter's consuming love which wins life for her daughter. Again, that same love underlies her "ill-content" and her consequent hope in "kindlier Gods" and in death's overthrow. Appropriately then, this new dispensation is envisioned in terms of love: an indifferent deity supplanted by a God of Love who will be worshiped not fearfully but lovingly. The conception is basically that which informs *In Memoriam:* the survival of love beyond death sustains faith in eternal life and defines God's nature as "Immortal Love."

VI Maud

In most dramatic monologues we encounter a speaker relating or indirectly revealing action in which he is still involved, at least emotionally. Demeter recalls the loss and recovery of her daughter; the hero of "Locksley Hall" reflects upon his disappointed love of shallow-hearted Amy. *Maud,* one of Tennyson's most original experiments, brings the speaker and his story still closer together by unfolding the action through a series of soliloquies that represent moments in its course. "The peculiarity of this poem," Tennyson said, "is that different phases of passion in one person take the place of different characters." [21] These different phases are expressed in soliloquies of various kinds: narrative, ruminative, lyrically effusive. It was a stroke of both descriptive and critical brilliance to have called *Maud,* as W. H. Auden did, "a libretto manqué." [22]

The "story" is sufficiently operatic: Tennyson's unnamed hero lives in solitude, brooding morosely over the financial ruin and suicide of his father and his mother's grief-stricken death. The return of Maud, proud young daughter of a neighboring family, breaks in upon the hero's morbid self-absorption. An agreement of their fathers, in an earlier period of mutual friendship, had destined Maud and the hero for each other; but this promise has long since lapsed and Maud's churlish brother now seems bent on marrying her to a milk-sop aristocrat. Maud and the young hero meet, however, and love grows between them. When Maud's brother interrupts a lovers' meeting, the hero kills him in a duel and flees. Maud dies of grief, and the hero suffers an interval of madness from which he is saved by the call to noble self-sacrifice in the Crimean War.

Tennyson called the poem—a favorite of his, which he delighted to read aloud to admiring visitors—"a little Hamlet"; and it also vibrates with echoes from melodramatic novels, especially Scott's *The Bride of Lammermoor*, the "spasmodic" poems of such leaders of that poetic vogue as Alexander Smith and Sidney Dobell, and Carlyle's *Sartor Resartus*. Recent research by Professor R. W. Rader has shown, however, that Maud is closely linked to Tennyson's own experience, most particularly to his brief, youthful attachment to Rosa Baring, a beauty of the Somersby neighborhood.[23] From a still different perspective, we may see in Tennyson's monodrama a kind of prophetic anticipation of the twentieth-century preoccupation with insanity as heroic gesture —an idea at least as old as Shakespeare and Cervantes but one that has particularly taken the literary fancy in our own era, from Strindberg to J. D. Salinger.

As an individual, Tennyson's hero is quite indistinct and unappealing; but then he is less a character than a scene of action: the essential drama takes place within the mind of the protagonist. It consists of a movement through successive "phases of passion" in response to the power of love. Of his hero, Tennyson said, "The poem is to show what love does for him";[24] and this purpose may be taken, though susceptible to sentimental reduction, as the basis of the poem's structure.

Part I, from its opening words, "I hate" to the culminating pitch of amatory expectancy in "Come into the garden, Maud," traces the hero's transformation—his awakening into life—under the spell of Maud's vivifying beauty and regard. The first lyric of this section expresses a mood of morbid scorn and radical disaffection. The hero's relentless enumerations of the repellent conditions of life as he has witnessed them makes the beginning of *Maud,* what a reviewer in *Blackwood's* said it is, a "screed of bombast"—perhaps one most appropriately read as a kind of Victorian equivalent of Allen Ginsberg's *Howl.* Compare its opening lines—

> I saw the best minds of my generation destroyed
> by madness, starving hysterical naked,
> dragging themselves through the negro streets at
> dawn looking for an angry fix. . . .[25]

—with some from Tennyson's *Maud:*

> And the vitriol madness flushes up in the ruffian's head,
> Till the filthy by-lane rings to the yell of the trampled wife,
> And chalk and alum and plaster are sold to the poor for bread,
> And the spirit of murder works in the very means of life.

But the social denunciation in *Maud* is permeated by bitter self-contempt:

> Sooner or later I too may passively take the print
> Of the golden age—why not? I have neither hope nor trust.

In this state the hero affects an extreme detachment as the only safeguard of his sanity, praying for "a passionless peace" and immunity from "the cruel madness of love." Yet love does come; though it is dreaded, like the coming of April to Eliot's wasteland, as a rekindling of memory and desire. The hero's suspicions yield to Maud's innocent grace; he seeks now not to be saved *from* love but to be saved *by* it. His realization that his beloved cares for him brings relief from the "lonely hell" of self-contempt: "But if *I* be dear to some one else,/Then I should be to myself more dear."

The hero's transformation is most strikingly revealed in the shifting attitude toward external nature he exhibits in the course of Part I. At the outset, the hero imputes to nature, by sinister and almost pathological personifications, a kind of willful malevolence. Later, the external world seems less the mirror of his troubled mind and asserts its own beauty. As his love shows signs of prospering, however, the hero looks anxiously to nature for some reflection of his hope (VI: "Morning arises stormy and pale, . . . I had fancied it would be fair"); and the "happy day" when their love is confessed does rival Maud herself in its beauty:

Rosy is the West
　　Rosy is the South,
Roses are her cheeks,
　　And a rose her mouth.
　　　　　　(Part I; XVII)

From this point to the end of Part I, nature has sprung to life in the eye of the transfigured hero: "A livelier emerald twinkles in the grass,/A purer sapphire melts into the sea" (Part XVIII, vi). The final lyric in Part I, "Come into the garden, Maud," completes with its famous *tour de force* of personification this metamorphosis. The spell that love has worked upon the hero is measured by the polar contrast between "the dreadful hollow behind the little wood," with its echoes of "Death" (Part I; I, i), and Maud's garden, a world that seems to exist only to contain and express the hero's rapture. Dominating this garden-world are the rose and the lily, those traditional emblems of beauty and purity that not only represent the heroine's charms ("Queen lily and rose in one") but more particularly epitomize the nature of Maud's dual influence upon the hero. He has been roused from a death-like emotional lethargy by a passion of which the rose is the symbol, and his cynicism has yielded in the presence of a true-hearted innocence whose floral equivalent Tennyson would again employ to characterize Elaine: "the lily maid of Astolat."

Though uneven in quality, Part I contains most of the poem's lyrical triumphs and constitutes a fully shaped and integral whole. There is less memorable poetry in Part II, and its more chaotic effect is not fully excused by the madness of the protagonist; Part III is perfunctory as a resolution of the "drama" and galling as an assertion of the meliorative influence of war. Tennyson's claims concerning the "holy power of love" at work upon his hero hardly apply to these last two sections, which follow the slaying of Maud's brother, unless the abrupt and unmotivated declaration that "I am one with my kind" on which note the poem ends could be considered a culmination of that theme.

The thematic adjunct of conflict undergoing a process of ennoblement is somewhat more satisfactorily fulfilled by the conclusion. At the beginning of the poem conflict is internal and wholly destructive; it takes the form of suicide in the hero's father and of course self-hatred and alienation in the hero—"At war with myself and a wretched race." In the social sphere, it is represented by the exploitation and predatory greed of a festering class struggle. The fatal duel has, for all its doleful consequences, at least the positive effect of drawing from both Maud's stricken brother and her lover the selfless admission that "The fault was mine." Conflict, at the poem's end, has become impersonal, almost abstract; and, as a "defence of the right," it is presented not as a divisive force but as a unifying one—a force that welds a nation together and binds the hero "to a cause that I felt to be pure and true."

Every reader must decide for himself whether the avid welcome to war with which *Maud* ends is tolerable. Of course, the speaker's sentiments are his own, not the poet's. Yet, argue as we will, the fact remains that the poem requires our assent to the hero's enthusiastic belief in "a hope for the world in the coming wars." There is no denying that "The blood-red blossom of war with a heart of fire" is deliberately proffered as a higher object for the passionate heart than the roses in Maud's garden. Such martial fervor, whatever might be said in its behalf, seems awkwardly framed in Tennyson's finely tuned numbers; the *poetry* of war, as Wilfred Owen said, is in the pity of it; and this would be true on grounds of esthetic decorum even without respect to what we consider enlightened sympathies.

There is so much in *Maud* upon which to base a claim to our interest—the originality of the "monodrama" conception, the element of oblique autobiography, the surprising acerbity of its social criticism, the often brilliant mastery of its common metrical forms—that it is a shame the whole is not more satisfying. Nor is it really possible, as it is with *In Memoriam,* to dismiss the chaff and treasure the wheat; for even the lyric gems of *Maud* are not detachable the way single cantos of Tennyson's great elegy are. Each lyric assumes, if not the dramatic situation, at least the *persona* that the total poem creates. It is a mark of Tennyson's skill, yet a curious limitation upon these lyrics, that their flavor does not quite survive separation from their context. Within this limitation, however, we *can* admire them singly, especially the simpler, less gaudy ones:

> O, let the solid ground
> Not fail beneath my feet
> Before my life has found

What some have found so sweet!
Then let come what come may,
What matter if I go mad,
I shall have had my day.

Let the sweet heavens endure,
Not close and darken above me
Before I am quite quite sure
That there is one to love me!
Then let come what come may,
To a life that has been so sad,
I shall have had my day.
(Part I; XI)

Though not among those poems most frequently praised, these lines show the kind of crystalline beauty by which readers of *Maud* are rewarded. The diction is so everyday and so predominantly monosyllabic, the sentiments are so nearly commonplace that the result could hardly be other than insipid; and yet somehow it is not. The simplicity is that of spare precision rather than slackness; poised on the brink of banality, the poem holds our wonder without acrobatics merely by refusing to plunge.

VII *The Plays*

In 1874, with his Arthurian epic all but complete and with most of his major achievements in the lyric, the short idyll, and the dramatic monologue well behind him, Tennyson—as one of his reviewers, the young Henry James, put it—"tempted fortune in the perilous field of the drama." [26] For a poet in his sixty-fifth year so novel an undertaking required considerable energy and no little resolution. The risk, which James himself would disastrously run in his own later years, was real enough, given Tennyson's morbid sensitivity to censure and the air of public anticipation with which each of the Laureate's dramatic productions would be received as "a great event for criticism as well as for poetry." [27] But behind this venture lay not so much a deliberate artistic conviction as the haphazard and even desperate way Tennyson tended to commit his talents in the face of flagging inspiration and a dearth of compelling subject matter.

To contemplate Tennyson's timid and derivative contribution to the drama in the light of Ibsen's and other Continental playwrights' nearly simultaneous wrenching of it in the direction of social realism provides an almost grotesque reminder of how irrelevant to the course of theatrical history Tennyson's plays were.[28] "The British drama," he complained, "must be in a low state indeed"; but he offered this assessment in explanation of unfriendly critics, not as a rallying cry against stale conventions and stifling inhibitions. His approach to the craft was almost wholly literary; the doctoring of his texts for stage production Tennyson was content to leave to professionals like Sir Henry Irving. Thus he evaded "the exigencies of our modern theatre," whereas dramatists with revolutionary vision would confront them as a challenge.

The mature Tennyson's career as a playwright occupied a period of some nine years and yielded seven plays. However, this accomplishment in poetic drama is at once enhanced and outshone by that work of remarkable precocity, *The Devil and the Lady,* an apparently unfinished play young Alfred amused himself with at about the age of fourteen (and which was not published until 1930).[29] A cheeky and delightful confection, *The Devil and the Lady* resembles a Jonsonian "humour" comedy more than anything else, but much of the verse has an almost Marlovian verve. It concerns the January-May marriage between Magus, an old necromancer, and Amoret, his frisky young wife. There is also a most likable though self-disparaging Devil, whom Magus conjures up to guard Amoret in his absence, and an array of suitors who speak entertainingly their various professional jargons: a lawyer, an apothecary, a sailor, an astronomer, a soldier, and a monk. "Methinks my tongue runs twenty knots an hour," exclaims the Devil at one point; he might truly be speaking on behalf of his young creator. The play is a deluge of juvenile pedantry and rhetorical figuration, a most thorough and impressive sowing of verbal wild oats.

For all the difference between *The Devil and the Lady* and the dramas Tennyson would write more than half a century later, they are similar in one essential respect: the youthful play and those of the old Laureate are all works of gifted mimicry rather than of authentic creative power. When it came to drama, Tennyson's ear was persistently cocked to literary echoes; he could neither approximate the sounds of actual speech nor convincingly embody the inner dialogue of the human passions.

Tennyson's chronicle plays form a triptych portraying, so the poet himself asserted, "the making of England." *Harold,* published in 1876, shows the awakening of a national consciousness and adumbrates the greatness of the English people as a composite race. *Becket,* the last of the three to be written, concerns the struggle of the Crown against the domination of the Church. In *Queen Mary,* the first to appear, this struggle ends with the downfall of Roman Catholicism in England and with the dawning of a new age marked by individual freedom.[30] Curiously, however, the protagonists and title characters of all three plays are champions of lost causes; their place is not as harbingers but among those who seem to resist the nation's destiny.

The growth of the playwright provides more interest in this case than the development of his theme, and for that reason Tennyson's histories are better considered in compositional rather than in chronological order. *Queen Mary,* which is more a historical pageant than a drama, is a crowded sequence of scenic highlights that touch vividly on the foreign and domestic turbulence, and religious animus, of a volatile and complex era of bad feeling. However, Tennyson's very concern about historical authenticity weighs the play down with inert detail and blurs its dramatic focus. After Archibishop Cranmer has been led away to the stake, Lords Howard and Paget hold the stage. "We talk and Cranmer suffers," says Howard; and the line might stand as a succinct diagnosis of what ails the play as a whole.

The Queen is a political force in the play and at times a commanding presence, but she never becomes a fully imagined character. In the dramatic high point, Cranmer's renunciation in St. Mary's Church before his execution, Queen Mary plays no part. Her love for the cold, unresponsive Philip of Spain, which is represented to be a tragic passion, seldom takes a more exalted form than petulant doting. The future of her realm is incidental; at the forefront again and again is Mary's desire to keep Philip by her side.

Harold has much more formal cohesion and dramatic interest, but its relation to "the making of England" theme is perhaps most tenuous of all three histories. The struggle between principle and necessity that grips the protagonist, though not conceived with great originality, is at least solidly and convincingly developed. At the outset, Harold stands, confident in his rectitude, as one who would rather "die than lie." But he is led painfully to experience how much more difficult it is to do the right than to profess it. What Tennyson hoped would resemble the force of doom[31] actually manifests itself as the tension generated by a moral dilemma.

The crucial scene in which Harold swears to help William gain the English crown, knowing he will break his oath, establishes the dilemma's dramatic validity. Both the pressures that urge Harold's promise and his resistance to them are well presented:

> *Wulfnoth.* Call it to temporize, and not to lie;
> Harold, I do not counsel thee to lie.
> The man that hath to foil a murderous aim
> May, surely, play with words.
> *Harold.* Words are the man.
> Not even for thy sake, brother, would I lie.
> (II, ii, 227–31)

In his subsequent alternations between self-contempt and self-justification the conflict is internalized and intensified. Harold's broken oath initiates a dramatic exploration of the question Stigand voices later in the play: "Is naked truth actable in true life?" (III, 1, 64). The protagonist's relation to this question is set off against that of the two other kings, Edward, his predecessor, and William, who conquers him. In Edward and William we see a kind of polarity: the Confessor's holiness is associated with a political ineffectualness that Tennyson had already shown as resulting from religious fanaticism in the *Idylls of the King;* William exemplifies the efficiency of ruthless opportunism. Harold's conscience-wracked expediency stands between these extremes. He cannot shirk public duty as does Edward, who has "A conscience for his own soul, not his realm"; neither can he shrug off moral issues with the callous realism of William.

The conflicting responsibilities that bear down upon Harold are appropriately reflected in the imagery of confinement and enclosure that permeates the play. Writhing in the toils of moral complexity, Harold longs for a lost world of simple, straightforward moral reflex in terms of physical openness and freedom: "O God, that I were in some wide, waste field/With nothing but my battle-axe and him/To spatter his brains!" (II, ii, 423–25). But this fantasy of decisive single combat is illusory; significantly, when Harold does finally face William in Senlac Field his chances depend upon the faithfulness of his men and their encircling wall of shields. Thus the fate of the Saxon forces symbolically reenacts Harold's moral tragedy: "Hot-headed fools—to burst the wall of shields!/They have broken the commandment of the king!"

Even before the battle at Senlac, however, Harold has begun to see that his responsibilities do not excuse him from being responsible, and that ends become tainted by their means: "Evil for good, it seems,/Is oft as childless of the good as evil/For evil" (V, i, 98–100). As a counter-statement to the "might makes right" principle which William's victory exemplifies, Harold's perception shows at least a glimmering of the tragic vision. Even though the Norman king figures more centrally in the making of England, the Saxon hero serves reasonably well in the making of drama.

In Thomas Becket, of course, Tennyson had a still finer protagonist; and, having gained considerably more mastery over the playwright's problems, he produced as his final history play a work that had enough genuine dramatic merit to make it a considerable stage success. The Laureate had learned, for one thing, to put history at the service of art rather than the reverse. Tennyson was not less careful about history in *Becket,* but he does show more skill in turning it to dramatic account. The chess game between Becket and Henry, with which the play begins, is an authentic touch gleaned from John of Salisbury; and Tennyson uses it with good effect as a foreshadowing of the contest in grim earnest between the King and the Archbishop. The crude methods of historical exposition that burden *Queen Mary* and persist in *Harold* are replaced by a Prologue that establishes the situation and smoothly initiates the action.

If Harold is torn between the right and the expedient, the conflict in *Becket* is the still more complex one of divided loyalties. Involved in the larger struggle of church and state are Becket's personal affinities, and Tennyson makes a fair show of bringing these into the drama. Both the Archbishop's fondness for Henry and his sense of duty to his office are convincing; Becket's popular sympathies give even the institutional clash the more human dimension of a conflict between civil order and the commonweal; and underlying all is the question of Thomas's commitment to what might be called the competing values of past and future—ecclesiastical tradition versus national destiny.

Yet, essentially, Tennyson's portrayal of Becket is less that of a man faced with rending choices than that of one consumed by spiritual pride. The playwright's own loyalties are divided, of course; he can hardly fail to be generous in the sympathetic characterization of his martyred hero, but Tennyson's anti-Roman inclinations and his religious liberalism are also indulged. Like the true saint, Becket does hunger after righteousness; but, like the soldier that he also is, he supposes that righteousness can only triumph in the total rout and humiliation of those who oppose it. John of Salisbury's warning that Thomas has raised the world against him leads to this revealing exchange:

Becket. Why, John, my kingdom is not of this world.
John of Salisbury. If it were more of this world it might be
More of the next. A policy of wise pardon
Wins here as well as there. To bless thine enemies—
Becket. Ay, mine, not Heaven's.
John of Salisbury. And may there not be something
Of this world's leaven in thee too . . . ?
(V, ii, 10–16)

Becket's identification of his personal cause with heaven's—a kind of spiritual solipsism—is the aspect of his pride that the play most tellingly exposes. Repeatedly, Becket's rhetoric equates the man himself with the power he serves: he *is* the King, he *is* the Pope, he *is* the Church and finally—in the martyrdom he all too readily invites—he *is* Christ.

Despite much in *Becket* that is well done, it does not bear extravagant admiration. A lack of thoroughness and clarity is especially evident in the dramatic rendering. Becket's change toward his king is only sketchily treated, and Tennyson takes too little advantage of the inherent possibilities for revealing the spiritual ordeal of his hero. Also, what *are* the truly decisive forces in Becket's martyrdom? Henry's struggle with the Church? The envy of the Barons? The hatred of Eleanor? There is more vagueness about the answer than need be. Finally, *Becket* shares with Tennyson's other chronicle plays a certain woodenness in characterization that accompanies the artificialities of his poetic dialogue. Too often his figures speak not as if they were making history but only as if they had read it.

After the historical trilogy Tennyson went on to lesser things. *The Falcon,* a one-act play, is based upon the familiar ninth tale of the fifth day in the *Decameron;* and in this work the Laureate does capture a promising sprightliness. Count Federigo, who has been beggared by love for the Lady Giovanna, discusses his desperate straits with Filippo, his foster-brother and factotum:

> *Count.* Come, come, Filippo, what is there in the larder?
> *Filippo.* Shelves and hooks, shelves and hooks, and when I see the shelves I am like to hang myself on the hooks.

But at length Tennyson's instinct plays him false, and the piece degenerates into sentimentality. "Stately and tender, isn't it?" he asked a friend who had listened to him read the manuscript. However, these qualities do not compensate for the irony which in Boccaccio is the life of the story but which Tennyson unhappily plays down.

On the other hand, irony is, if anything, overworked in *The Cup,* an attempt at something like Classical tragedy that suffers by the comparison—particularly with Aeschylus's *Agamemnon*—it evokes. The story, taken from Plutarch, concerns the vengeance of Camma upon Synorix, her lustful and devious pursuer, for the murder of her husband. Synorix, having drunk from the poisoned cup Camma shares with him at their marriage ceremony, calls their deaths a work of the Fates—a tragedy beyond individual guilt; but we could not believe him even if he were not such a scoundrel. There is no sense of cosmic forces at work, only at best the rusty machinery of inferior revenge tragedy.

Charity might allow *The Foresters* as a nostalgic old man's pastoral pipe dream. Tennyson's simple-hearted delight in the doings of Robin Hood and Maid Marian would be almost touching if the artistic result were less painfully bad:

> *Marian.* Earl—
> *Robin.* Nay, no Earl am I. I am English yeoman.
> *Marian.* Then *I* am yeo-woman. O the clumsy word!

As for the plot, it conforms almost uncannily to the threadbare traditions of nineteenth-century melodrama. This characteristic can be seen from the following speech, the banality of which gives also an even better sample of the play's style than the lines quoted above:

Marian. Ah, well! thou seest the land has come between us,
And my sick father here has come between us,
And this rich Sheriff too has come between us;
So, is it not all over now between us?

Withal, *The Foresters* may be seen as a kind of feeble antithesis to the *Idylls of the King*. An absent king returns, and the old order is restored. Robin, who shares the Arthurian virtues with King Richard (or, alternatively, is a loyal counterpart to the traitorous Lancelot), is united with a faithful maid. The pessimism of the *Idylls*, so evident even Tennyson himself feared he had overdone it, is countered here with an optimism so jejune as to be anything but reassuring. If brooding uncertainty was inherent in Tennyson's nature, so was the compulsion to proclaim—whether from the deeps of *In Memoriam* or the shallows of *The Foresters*—that "all is well."

Tennyson's last play, *The Promise of May*, is another melodrama. The villain, Mr. Philip Edgar, mouths political and moral sentiments of an "advanced" kind; but the relation to modern issues is superficial: the rural setting and the dramatis personae come from the dusty attic of Tennyson's English Idyls. Edgar, who seduces one of Farmer Dobson's two daughters and returns five years later to court the other, seems initially more of a Pateresque seeker after intense moments than a person of strong radical convictions. Upon his reappearance he displays the sated and guilt-plagued manner of a bogus Byronism. Tennyson regarded the play as "a drama of character"; and the Marquis of Queensbury, a self-proclaimed "secularist and freethinker," was in fact sufficiently affected to denounce the production, during its brief run in 1882, both from the audience and in the press, as an abominable attack upon those of his persuasion. However, it is strange to think of anyone's taking *The Promise of May* or any of the characters in it so seriously, which is not to deny that its blatant Philistinism—especially Farmer Dobson's crusty contempt for artists, books, and schoolmasters—is still annoying.

But the concluding word should not go to this unfortunate work. At a time when Tennyson had neither youthful energy nor a hunger for recognition to spur him, and when current fashions in the theater had less than nothing of value to teach, Tennyson, though he did not reform the English theater of the period, achieved with his histories—or the best of them, *Becket*—closet drama that can stand comparison to anything nineteenth-century England produced in that category. Admittedly, however, it is not a comparison many readers are avid to explore.

CHAPTER 5

The Achievement

And yet it may be better, if we must,
To find the stance impressive and absurd
Than not to see the hero for the dust.[1]
Donald Davie

As a young man, Tennyson looked to Edward FitzGerald "something like Hyperion shorn of his beams"; in age he struck one visitor as "a dilapidated Jove." The godlike quality was not to be denied, but it seemed compounded with a disconcerting quantity of mortal dross. What his acquaintances encountered in the man thoughtful critics have usually found in the poetry: impressive features accompanied by some fundamental lack that not only limits admiration but seems to call it essentially into question. Many a lesser poet may be praised more comfortably than Tennyson; and, as a result, most general critical estimates—even when sympathetic—have taken more frequently the form of clinical diagnosis than appreciative analysis. Several of these diagnoses are excellent; and the student of Tennyson may be referred to the opinions of W. H. Auden, Paull Baum, F. L. Lucas, and Harold Nicolson with the assurance that, by a bit of winnowing and syncretizing, he will have the essential case thoroughly and discerningly set before him.[2]

That Tennyson ranks as a major poet is both an obvious and, in itself, not very illuminating conclusion. However, the way in which the fact requires us to regard Tennyson's poetry does tend to clarify the nature of his achievement. In a certain sense Tennyson would be a major poet if only because of his unprecedented popularity among his contemporaries and the large place he assumed in Victorian culture. But he has sounder, more intrinsic claims. A recent authority has enumerated the "essential attributes of majority: dedication to the poet's calling, command of his medium, range of vision, capacity for growth, magnitude of performance, and place in a tradition" [3]—and he concludes that Tennyson qualifies in all respects. T. S. Eliot calls Tennyson "a great poet" because of his abundance, variety, and complete competence.[4] Such views command assent, but they appeal not to our sense of wonder and wholehearted admiration but to our reason, our sense of justice and proportion. "Of course Tennyson is a great poet—or anyway a major one!" we reply. "What else would he be?" In truth, however, we would like Tennyson better if we could take him as a minor poet, rediscovering his splendors with gratitude and neglecting his inanities with a clear conscience. But this is not really possible in the long run; Tennyson *is* inescapably a major, even a great poet, yet in many important ways a disappointing one. His very stature is an inconvenience.

To say so is to modify slightly yet perhaps crucially the notion of Tennyson as a flawed divinity. The true Olympians of art are at their best when attempting the most difficult challenge; their imperfections are transcended, not underscored, by what Keats speaks of as "godlike hardship." With Tennyson it was otherwise: his great undertakings do exhibit some of his most memorable felicities, but they also expose his worst failings—excessive ornateness in the *Idylls of the King,* moral obtuseness and an inclination to bathos in *Maud,* a substitution of literal for imaginative truth in the history plays, and a weakness for banal sermonizing in *In Memoriam.* The works in which Tennyson's gifts show to best advantage are those that are somehow circumscribed—by the properties of the given occasion, by the possibilities of the literary source, or by the proprieties of the chosen mood. Tennyson's "divinity" therefore is itself a flaw; that is to say, Tennyson at his most ambitious is not Tennyson at his best. That is hardly what we feel about major poets in general. Perhaps it explains as well as anything else why critical attacks on Tennyson are usually so lacking in charity—why their tone suggests not "Homer nods" but "the Emperor is naked."

It is tempting to conclude, as many have, that because in Professor Baum's phrase, "his grasp exceeded his reach," [5] Tennyson's was a case of misdirected talent. The values and tastes of the age were uncongenial, if not bad in themselves, a common view has held; and Tennyson was corrupted by his age. Recent criticism has begun to question this judgment on various grounds; but, even if we agree that it was bad for Tennyson to be so much a part of his age, the even more striking fact is that, in essential ways, he appears to have been disastrously out of touch with it. Timid and moody by nature and swathed in adulation and bland domesticity, Tennyson—for all his earnest reading of Lyell and Max Müller, his scientific dabbling, his membership in the Metaphysical Society, and his acquaintance with a variety of eminent minds—simply lived a life largely removed from the yeasty social turmoil of his times and from the genuine sources of intellectual novelty and challenge. To cite the emotional sensitivity of *In Memoriam* as evidence of his grasp of scientific ideas or to recall that Huxley himself thought Tennyson "the first poet since Lucretius who understood the drift of science," does not really alter the case. Tennyson allowed himself to become, as Henry James discovered, estranged from "the great adventure of sensibility" that his times offered.

Unlike Tennyson's own Ulysses, he was not avid for novel experiences; he resented any probing of his convictions as an invasion of privacy, and he sometimes cringed from the exposure of intellectual give and take. Far from becoming a part of all he met, his usual program with company was to take his guests up to his study; overwhelm them in tobacco smoke; and—saying "Let me read you *Maud;* you'll never forget it"—hypnotize them with his strange, deep, chanting renditions of his poems. These quirks would hardly deserve notice except that Tennyson's poetry so often reflects just this lack of gusto, of imaginative involvement with and full awareness of the world around him. It is precisely the opposite of Keats's "negative capability"; rather than the capacity of being *in* uncertainties without any irritable reaching after fact and reason, Tennyson's inclination was either to "stretch lame hands of faith, and grope,/And gather dust and chaff" or to stand apart and pontificate *about* uncertainty.

> Flower in the crannied wall,
> I pluck you out of the crannies,
> I hold you here, root and all, in my hand,
> Little flower—but *if* I could understand
> What you are, root and all, and all in all,
> I should know what God and man is.

One authority has said this little poem "concentrates into six lines the Hegelian doctrine that the object to be understood in its full particularity has a fixed but ever-changing relation to the totality of the becoming universe." [6] It may be so; but, as imagined experience rather than philosophical doctrine, the poem gives us an uprooted flower and a bemused poet who has murdered—not even to dissect, but to puzzle over the futility of dissection. This, as William Blake might have told him, is how *not* to see a heaven in a wild flower.

But Blake—and Keats at his greatest—were literalists of the imagination, whereas Tennyson's truest instincts and powers were those of the decorative poet. He was neither visionary nor inventive, and he possessed little of imagination's rarest gift: the power of sympathy. Consequently, we often feel he has not revealed the beauty or significance inherent in the object or situation but has, rather, embellished it with "fine touches." Ruskin classified Tennyson among the "emotional" poets, behind those of "the first or creative class," and supposed that "if he could conceive more he would describe less." [7]

Decoration, however, is not merely a matter of pictorial flourishes. It is also manifested by the brilliant application of craft to a particular experience or occasion, aiming at a poem that, in contrast to Shelley's analogy of the fading coal with its implication of the artistically uncapturable, enhances the moment with its ideal formal framing. Such are Tennyson's several epigrammatic or epistolary tributes like "The Roses on the Terrace" and "To Mary Boyle"; such too is the graceful poem on Catullus, "'Frater Ave atque Vale,'" and in a quite different way "Sir Launcelot and Queen Guinevere." Even some of Tennyson's more "personal" poems have, as their chief distinction, this cool, assured elegance.

It is as curious as it is regrettable, then, that in Tennyson such splendid decorative skill should have been conjoined with its most unlikely handicap: a deficiency of taste. If, as Valerie Pitt suggests, Victorianism deserves some of the blame,[8] at least it did not initiate what Harold Nicolson calls Tennyson's lack of emotional delicacy.[9] Signs that his taste was inherently erratic appear in poems written before not only Tennyson, but the age itself, was Victorian. Consider an example from that lively piece of juvenilia, *The Devil and the Lady.* The young wife Amoret weeps in fear before the Devil, who says:

> Is that a tear which stains thy cheek? Nay—now
> It quivers at the tip-end of thy nose
> Which makes it somewhat dubious from which feature
> It first had issue.

Young Tennyson is having fun here mimicking Elizabethan dialogue, and no doubt a touch of boyish coarseness is preferable to the "Schoolmiss Alfred" manner. But there is a bit more snide cleverness than belongs to the honest charm of boyhood. Of course what makes the Devil's allusion to a runny nose offensive is its incongruity. The reference obtrudes upon the dramatic situation an element that nullifies the fright of Amoret and is unworthy of the Devil's proper courtliness. It is wholly gratuitous.

The absence of taste, however, is not always marked by a lapse into crudeness; the insipid, the sentimental, the sententious, or the excessively ornate may do even more violence to decorum. Wherever Tennyson takes a turn that seems to blur the conception or to jar against the dominant effect we sense this weakness. In the early poem "The Deserted House," the macabre allegory of a human skull when "Life and Thought have gone away" is damaged in one way by mention of the vacant dwelling's door having once been "So frequent on its hinge," and in another by the conclusion in which Life and Thought are said to have moved to "A mansion incorruptible" in a "city glorious." The result is an unappetizing mixture of ghoulishness, satire, and piety.

Again, we have the deplorable sections of "Guinevere" where Arthur makes high-minded pronouncements over the prostrate form of his humiliated queen are essentially a failure of taste. Similarly, the frequent imagery in *In Memoriam* which expresses the poet's love of his dead friend in terms of saccharine domesticity. Instances are varied, yet they have in common some quality of the unassimilable—and the insensitivity that allows it—that is the characteristic of bad taste. When the poet protests that his lady "All my bounding heart entanglest/In a golden-netted smile" ("Madeline"), we can charge such an awkward and distracting figure to the inexperience and extravagance of youth. But when he spoils a seasoned performance by speaking of Virgil as "Wielder of the stateliest measure ever moulded by the lips of man," we must conclude that his ear was keener to the sounds and rhythms of words than was his mind's eye to the ideas those words might conjure up. Yet Tennyson is less often guilty of violating our sense of visual congruity than he is of exhibiting a certain failure of tact. To speak of "The blood-red blossom of war" is obtuse in almost any context, and to close the pathetic story of Enoch Arden by stressing the costliness of his funeral even more obviously misses the mark. Gerard Manley Hopkins dismissed "Locksley Hall" as "an ungentlemanly row" [10]—an odd and irrelevant description on the face of it. Nonetheless, it touches the vulnerable point—assuming Hopkins's sense of the "gentlemanly" was Newman's: ". . . a cultivated intellect, a delicate taste, a candid, equitable, dispassionate mind . . ." (*The Idea of a University*).

Yet after all, to quote Newman again, "one idea is not another idea"; and the idea of a gentleman can have only a limited bearing upon the achievement of a poet. Our leave-taking might better turn from such considerations to a final glance at a particular example of the poetry itself, since far as a sampling may be from a summing up, we sense what a poet *is* less from the accumulation of all that he did than from what especially and supremely he *could do*. Tennyson's stipulation that "Crossing the Bar" be placed at the end of all editions of his poems has invited readers to regard it as an ultimate poetic statement; in any event, it is a splendid and characteristic lyric (though, like its author, popularly esteemed more because it expresses noble feelings than because it does so with rare art). Moreover, as one commentator has suggested, it presents a succinct display of Tennyson's typical strengths and weaknesses in revealing conjunction:[11]

Sunset and evening star,
  And one clear call for me!
And may there be no moaning of the bar,
  When I put out to sea,

But such a tide as moving seems asleep,
  Too full for sound and foam,
When that which drew from out the boundless deep
  Turns again home.

Twilight and evening bell,
  And after that the dark!
And may there be no sadness of farewell,
  When I embark;

For tho' from out our bourne of Time and Place
    The flood may bear me far,
I hope to see my Pilot face to face
    When I have crost the bar.

"Crossing the Bar" has that sheen of eloquence which gives much of Tennyson's poetry an immediate and forceful appeal. The stateliness of its movement is sustained by rhythmic variations from stanza to stanza that do not, however, obscure the close similarity between the first and third and the second and fourth stanzas. This balance underscores the elaborate parallel in imagery and subject between the first half of the poem and the second. References to its "integrity," its "self-sustained completeness," are thus amply justified, as is the discovery in its plangent harmonies of "a quiet faith expressed in the perfect peace of a controlled art." [12]

But extended scrutiny can bring elements of the poem to notice and raise questions of tone and meaning that tend to dim its luster. Do the last two stanzas develop from the first two, or do they merely echo them? Is the theme thereby enriched or simply made more explicit? One critic is led to these questions by a study of the correspondences between the poem's two halves and sums up his sense of Tennyson's failure in execution by saying: "metaphor has been reduced to simile." [13] The idea of a reunion with God being likened to meeting the ship's pilot face to face bothers many thoughtful readers. The image lacks majesty, and it is forced to work on the figurative level in a way that seems out of keeping with the specific function of the literal pilot. Even the serene faith that makes "Crossing the Bar" a funereal standby has been drastically qualified and in fact denied: the poet's "hope" is not affirmation but a sign of his "life-long dubiety"; [14] the poem's essential tone is that of "depression and gloom." [15] If not, at least the poem exhibits in its conflicting identification of the source of being with both "the boundless deep" and "my Pilot" a "characteristically Tennysonian" confusion between "a god 'more or less' anthropomorphic and pantheism 'of a sort.' " [16]

Such is the damaging report—not altogether lacking in conflicts of its own—that modern literary analysis makes upon "Crossing the Bar." It is no unfair example of the kind of fate a good many of Tennyson's poems meet when subjected to probing, unsentimental criticism. Nevertheless, if we return to the poem still willing to let it work its power, we find that the damage is not so fundamental as it had seemed. Some of the flaws are real, but the critics with their own ideas of what the poem should be doing may not see what the poem really does; they have not taken Tennyson's measure. Most of their objections reflect the underlying assumption that the oppositions in the poem are inadvertent and inept inconsistencies: between faith and doubt, between the cosmic and the mundane, or between the symbolic and suggestive and the literal and overt. However, these opposing elements, insofar as they do exist in the poem, are not polarized but interwoven in a functional way. They are, in fact, variations or extensions of the fundamental alternation that permeates and organizes the poem: an alternation that defines the mood in which the approach of death is contemplated.

This mood is one that combines a sense of the mysterious, the unknown, the vast, and the ominous with a sense of the familiar, the natural, and the welcome. Individual words, corresponding lines, and the balancing halves of the poem all serve rather intricately to develop this combination. That "Crossing the Bar" presents death as both a summons and a reunion, both a voyage into the grim unknown and a homecoming, both a return to the primordial and a friendly meeting need not perplex us if we understand it not in terms of intellectual speculations or convictions but as a recreation of emotional experience, whose controlling tension is introduced by the opening words of the poem. "Sunset and evening star"—the day's end brings with it dark but also its own reassuring beacon. The star—and in a different way the evening bell in the third stanza—mingles the vast with the enduring, distance with presence. Such imagery may be "transparent"—Tennyson is both strong and vulnerable when dealing in these elemental simplicities—but its remarkable aptness makes it ring true.

Notes and References

Preface

1. Nancy M. Engbretsen, "Tennyson and Modernism," *Arts and Sciences* (New York University Bulletin), LXVII (Winter, 1965), 33.

Chapter One

1. *Further Letters of Gerard Manley Hopkins,* ed. Claude Colleer Abbott (London, 1938), p. 68.
2. Hallam Lord Tennyson, *Alfred Lord Tennyson: A Memoir,* (New York, 1897), I, 12.
3. *Memoir,* I, 35.
4. Sir Harold Nicolson, *Tennyson: Aspects of His Life, Character and Poetry* (Boston, 1925), p. 120.
5. Quoted in Paull F. Baum, *Tennyson Sixty Years After* (Chapel Hill, 1948), p. 39.
6. *Edinburgh Review,* LXXVII (1843), 373–91, 391.
7. *Letters of Edward Fitzgerald* (London, 1894), I, 273–78.
8. *The Letters of Elizabeth Barrett Browning,* ed. Kenyon (New York, 1910), I, 345, 367.
9. *Memoir,* I, 303.
10. *Memoir,* II, 350.
11. *Memoir,* II, 172.
12. Quoted by Baum, p. 25.
13. *Memoir,* I, 145.
14. Paul Elmer More, *Shelburne Essays, Seventh Series* (New York, 1910), p. 65.
15. *The Complete Works of Algernon Charles Swinburne,* ed. Gosse and Wise (London, 1926), XVI, 405.
16. Henry James, *The Middle Years* (London, 1917), pp. 86, 90, 104.
17. Nicolson, p. 27.
18. Nicolson, p. 15.
19. See E. D. H. Johnson, *The Alien Vision of Victorian Poetry* (Princeton, 1952); Jerome Hamilton Buckley, "The Two Voices" in *The Victorian Temper* (Cambridge, 1951); Elton Edward Smith, *The*

Two Voices: A Tennyson Study (Lincoln, Nebraska, 1964); Clyde de L. Ryals, *Theme and Symbol in Tennyson's Poems to 1850* (Philadelphia, 1964), p. 7; Arthur J. Carr, "Tennyson as a Modern Poet," *University of Toronto Quarterly,* XIX (1950), 368; and Valerie Pitt, *Tennyson Laureate* (Toronto, 1963), p. 18.

20. Herbert Marshall McLuhan, "Introduction," *Alfred Lord Tennyson: Selected Poetry* (New York, 1956).

21. Carr, p. 361.

22. Ryals, p. 7.

23. Jerome Hamilton Buckley, *Tennyson: The Growth of a Poet* (Cambridge, 1960), pp. viii, 253–56.

24. Valerie Pitt, *Tennyson Laureate,* and Joanna Richardson, *The Pre-Eminent Victorian* (London, 1962).

25. Ralph Wilson Rader, *Tennyson's* Maud: *The Biographical Genesis* (Berkeley, 1963), p. 121.

Chapter Two

1. Quoted in *Memoir,* I, 50.

2. Sir Charles Tennyson, *Alfred Tennyson* (New York, 1949), p. 33.

3. *Memoir,* I, 17.

4. George O. Marshall, Jr., in "Tennyson's 'The Poet': Mis-seeing Shelley Plain," *Philological Quarterly,* XL (1961), 156–57, points out, however, that Shelly's *Defence of Poetry* was not published until ten years after Tennyson's poem. Of course, Shelley's poetry, which Sir Charles Tennyson (*Alfred Tennyson,* p. 34) believes Tennyson to have made his first acquaintance with at Cambridge, might have been an influence on a poem published in 1830.

5. *The Devil and the Lady and Unpublished Poems,* edited by Sir Charles Tennyson (Bloomington, Indiana, 1964). Hereafter cited as *UEP.*

6. Clyde de L. Ryals, *Theme and Symbol in Tennyson's Poems to 1850,* p. 114.

7. An explication of the poem as an illustration of "the radical ambivalence of Tennyson's attitude towards the poetic life" is undertaken by G. Robert Stange in "Tennyson's Garden of Art: A Study of *The Hesperides,*" *Publications of the Modern Language Association,* LXVII (1952), 732–43.

8. "The Palace of Art," 1. 180.

9. See, for example, F. R. Leavis, *New Bearings in English Poetry* (London, 1961), p. 16.

10. *Memoir,* II, 92.

11. *Unpublished Letters of Matthew Arnold,* ed. Arnold Whitridge (New Haven, 1923), p. 17.

12. For a quite different impression of this poem see Ryals, *Theme and Symbol*, pp. 134–36.
13. W. H. Auden, "Introduction," *A Selection from the Poems of Alfred, Lord Tennyson* (Garden City, 1944), p. xvi.
14. Much of the material in this section (and some in the section on *In Memoriam* that follows it) is drawn from my essay, "Tennyson: The Passion of the Past and the Curse of Time," *ELH, A Journal of English Literary History*, XXXII (1965), 85–109.
15. *Memoir*, II, 319.
16. Sir James Knowles, "Aspects of Tennyson: A Personal Reminiscence," *The Nineteenth Century*, XXXIII (1893), 170.
17. *Memoir*, I, 154.
18. *Memoir*, I, 171–72.
19. "Tennyson's Poems," *Early Essays of John Stuart Mill*, ed. J. W. M. Gibbs (London, 1897), p. 242. This essay originally appeared in the *London Review*, July, 1835.
20. Printed in *Memoir*, I, 161.
21. Andrew Lang, *Alfred Tennyson* (Edinburgh and London, 1901), p. 51.
22. *Memoir*, I, 253.
23. Wordsworth, "Lines Composed a few miles above Tintern Abbey on revisiting the banks of the Wye during a tour. July 13, 1798," ll. 138–39, 141–42.
24. The shift I have in mind is described by Georges Poulet in *Studies in Human Time*, tr. Elliot Coleman (Baltimore, 1956), pp. 25–29.
25. *Memoir*, II, 73.
26. *Memoir*, I, 11.
27. *The Lover's Tale*, l. 157. In his chapter titled "Shadow and Substance," in *The Alien Vision of Victorian Poetry*, E. D. H. Johnson discusses the place of dreams, trances, and other "planes of irrational consciousness" in Tennyson's poetry. See also Sir Charles Tennyson, "The Dream in Tennyson's Poetry." *The Virginia Quarterly Review*, XL, No. 2 (1964), 228–48.
28. "Gareth and Lynette," ll. 272–74.
29. "The Day-Dream," l. 168.
30. *Memoir*, II, 364.
31. T. S. Eliot, "*In Memoriam*," *Essays Ancient and Modern* (New York, 1936), p. 196.
32. On the other hand, the poem does make reference to moments of communion with the dead (most notably in Canto XCV), but whatever the spiritual significance of such fleeting mystical moments, they do not negate the kind of natural separation upon which Tennyson so repeatedly dwells.

33. Paull F. Baum, *Tennyson Sixty Years After,* p. 125.
34. "To J. S.," 1. 17.
35. *Essays Ancient and Modern,* p. 197.
36. For example, in XX, XL, LX, LXII, LXIV, and XCVII.
37. Eleanor Mattes, *In Memoriam: The Way of a Soul* (New York, 1951), p. 61.

Chapter Three

1. *"In Memoriam," Essays Ancient and Modern,* p. 192.
2. See H. M. McLuhan, "Tennyson and the Romantic Epic," *Critical Essays on the Poetry of Tennyson,* ed. John Killham (London, 1960), pp. 86–95.
3. *Maud* is discussed in Chapter 4 under dramatic poetry, but the genesis of its "plot" in a single lyric and the way intervening action is implied rather than rendered seem to me matters related to the subject of narrative technique.
4. *"In Memoriam," Essays Ancient and Modern,* p. 191.
5. Herbert Marshall McLuhan, "Tennyson and the Romantic Epic" (in Killham), p. 94.
6. Tennyson commonly used this spelling to distinguish his English Idyls from *Idylls of the King.*
7. Jerome Hamilton Buckley, *Tennyson: The Growth of a Poet,* p. 80.
8. The evidence is conscientiously analyzed in R. W. Rader, *Tennyson's* Maud: *The Biographical Genesis,* especially pp. 30–31, 47–49.
9. On Biedermeier as "the dominant note, the background, the unfailing ingredient" of the art and literature of the nineteenth century, see Mario Praz, *The Hero in Eclipse in Victorian Fiction* (London, 1956), especially pp. 117–18, n. 4.
10. *Memoir,* I, 248, n. 1.
11. W. P. Ker, *Collected Essays* (London, 1925), I, 268.
12. Paull F. Baum's chapter on *The Princess* (*Tennyson Sixty Years After,* pp. 98–104) is an excellent appreciation of the poem's comedy.
13. Allan Danzig, "Tennyson's *The Princess:* A Definition of Love," *Victorian Poetry,* IV (Spring, 1966), 83–89, anticipates many of the points discussed here, though he regards the development of the main characters as more philosophical than psychological.
14. Lionel Stevenson, "The 'High-Born Maiden' Symbol in Tennyson," *Publications of the Modern Language Association,* LXII (March–June, 1948), 234–43, remarks upon the "amazing precision" with which the "high-born maiden" figure in Tennyson's poems conforms "to the theory of Jung regarding the archetypal image of the *anima.*" Stevenson and subsequent commentators (see especially J. H. Buckley,

Tennyson, p. 101) have applied Jung's conception of the *anima* to Ida's relationship to the Prince, though perhaps not pushing the application as far as I do here. Buckley calls the Princess "the projection of Tennyson's own aesthetic vision and conflict." With due regard for W. H. Auden's warning that "no other poet is easier, and less illuminating, to psychoanalyze," I would nevertheless add that, in view of the fact that the period of the poem's planning and composition coincides with the trying years of Tennyson's courtship and engagement, personal as well as esthetic conflict is reflected in *The Princess*.

15. The only substantial incident involving either of these friends, Cyril's singing of the bawdy song, is curiously suggestive of a certain dissonance in Tennyson himself. Edmund Gosse recorded that in a conversation with the Archbishop of Canterbury concerning "the distinction between grossness of speech and immorality in life" the Archbishop cited Tennyson as an example—"so coarse a talker and of a life so noble." (Quoted in Paul F. Matthiesen, "Gosse's Candid 'Snapshots'," *Victorian Studies*, VIII [June, 1965], 343.)

16. Frederic Harrison, *Tennyson, Ruskin, Mill and Other Literary Estimates* (New York, 1900), p. 20.

17. Paull F. Baum, *Tennyson, Sixty Years After*, p. 208.

18. Ernest Renan, "The Poetry of the Celtic Races," *Harvard Classics*, XXXII, 103.

19. *Memoir*, II, 122.

20. Sir Edward Strachey, "Introduction" to the Globe Edition of *Morte d'Arthur* (London, 1868), pp. xxxvi–xxxvii.

21. Sir Harold Nicolson, *Tennyson* (New York: Anchor Books, 1962), p. 323.

22. Clyde de L. Ryals argues in his stimulating essay, "The Moral Paradox of the Hero in *Idylls of the King*," *ELH, A Journal of English Literary History*, XXX (1963) 53–69, that Arthur's very ideality does, indeed, make him "both the hero and the villain of the *Idylls of the King*." This, it seems to me, gives more validity to the arguments of the "false" characters than Tennyson would have allowed, even though (and this is one of the redeeming features of the epic) Tennyson does not scant the psychological, rhetorical, and dramatic force of such arguments. Professor Ryals's essay is reprinted in his book *From the Great Deep: Essays on the Idylls of the King* (Athens, Ohio, 1967), a volume devoted to making the strongest possible case for the *Idylls* as a complex philosophical poem.

23. *Memoir*, I, 456–57.

24. I am conscious of stretching these hard-worked terms, "irony" and "paradox," in using them to refer not simply to rhetorical devices but to the governing outlooks that generate them. Whatever further

refinements a really adequate consideration of their distinctions and similarities as rhetorical and imaginative modes might require, I take it in any case that irony stresses the *falseness of* appearances and is hence inherently negative, whereas paradox stresses a *truth beneath* appearances and is therefore generally affirmative. For a different response to the abundant paradoxes and ironies in the *Idylls,* see Stanley J. Solomon, "Tennyson's Paradoxical King," *Victorian Poetry,* I (1963), 258–72.

25. "In Harmony with Nature."

26. F. E. L. Priestley, "Tennyson's *Idylls," Critical Essays on the Poetry of Tennyson,* ed. John Killham, p. 249. I should like to acknowledge my very considerable debt to this persuasive and illuminating essay (which was originally published in the *University of Toronto Quarterly,* XIX [1949], 35–49). It provides an excellent basis for appreciating the solidity of Tennyson's ethical vision in the poem: ". . . it is the essence of ethics to be not descriptive, but normative; not to tell us how we behave, but how we ought to behave. The ethics of naturalism confuse the prescriptive end of ethics with the descriptive end of science" (Killham, p. 250).

27. See especially Paull Baum, *Tennyson, Sixty Years After,* p. 212.

28. See Priestey, p. 250.

29. Baum, p. 191.

30. Nicolson (Anchor ed), p. 328.

31. René Girard, *Deceit, Desire, and the Novel: Self and Other in Literary Structure,* tr. Yvonne Freccero (Baltimore, 1965), p. 2. Girard's chapter on "Triangular Desire" has a number of very suggestive applications to the ethical conceptions Tennyson is working with in the *Idylls.*

32. *Ibid.,* p. 4.

33. See the "Author's Preface" to Henry Fielding's *Joseph Andrews.*

34. Cited by Girard in *Deceit, Desire, and the Novel,* p. 5.

35. Compare the *Idylls'* great rival among Victorian poems of epic scope, *The Ring and the Book.* Browning, as Henry James's observations on the novelistic qualities of *The Ring and the Book* recognized, is "novelizing" the long poem; Tennyson, on the other hand (his typical method of first writing out a prose paraphrase of a particular idyll and then versifying it signifies as much), is "poetizing" the narrative.

36. "The *Quartet:* Two Reviews," *The World of Lawrence Durrell,* ed. Harry T. Moore (Carbondale, Ill., 1962), p. 206.

37. Lionel Trilling, "Manners, Morals, and the Novel," *The Liberal Imagination* (New York, 1953), p. 206.

Chapter Four

1. *Memoir,* II, 319.
2. Quoted in *The Complete Poetical Works of Tennyson,* ed. W. J. Rolfe (Cambridge, 1898), p. 260.
3. *The Works of Tennyson,* ed. Hallam Tennyson (London, 1908), II, 376.
4. *Memoir,* II, 255.
5. Paull F. Baum, *Tennyson Sixty Years After,* p. 149.
6. Jerome Hamilton Buckley, *Tennyson: The Growth of a Poet.* p. 219.
7. Richard Hengist [Henry] Horne, ed., *A New Spirit of the Age* (London, 1907), p. 249. The *New Spirit* was originally published in 1844.
8. Douglas Bush, *Mythology and the Romantic Tradition,* (Cambridge, 1937), 205–206.
9. W. W. Robson, "The Dilemma of Tennyson," in *Critical Essays on the Poetry of Tennyson,* ed. John Killham, p. 159.
10. *Memoir,* I, 196.
11. See E. J. Chiasson, "Tennyson's 'Ulysses'—a Re-interpretation," in *Critical Essays on the Poetry of Tennyson,* p. 168.
12. Matthew Arnold, "The Function of Criticism at the Present Time."
13. *Memoir,* I, 135.
14. Buckley, *Tennyson,* p. 62.
15. I am anticipated here by E. D. H. Johnson, *The Alien Vision of Victorian Poetry,* p. 13.
16. "The Palace of Art," l. 197.
17. *Memoir,* II, 337.
18. Walter Pater's essay on "The Myth of Demeter and Persephone," published in the *Fortnightly Review* some thirteen years before Tennyson's poem (reprinted in *Greek Studies* [London, 1910], pp. 81–93), interprets the myth in terms of the same three levels of significance—natural, emotional, and ethical—as does the poem. On Victorian theories of mythological interpretation, see my essay, "Victorian Mythology," *Victorian Studies,* VI (1962), 5–28. The present discussion of "Demeter and Persephone" is adapted from the concluding pages of this article. See also G. Robert Stange, "Tennyson's Mythology: A Study of *Demeter and Persephone,*" *ELH, A Journal of English Literary History,* XXI (1954), 71.
19. *Memoir,* II, 364.
20. George Cox, *An Introduction to the Science of Comparative Mythology and Folklore* (New York, 1881), p. 353. Similar interpretations may be found in George Grote, *History of Greece* (New York,

1856), I, 41, and in Pater, *Greek Studies,* p. 114. Note that Tennyson's phrase "the desolate mother" (l. 72) suggests the *mater dolorosa* parallel both Grote and Pater mention.

21. *Memoir,* I, 396.

22. W. H. Auden, "Introduction," *A Selection from the Poems of Alfred, Lord Tennyson,* p. xiv, n. 2.

23. Ralph W. Rader, *Tennyson's* Maud: *The Biographical Genesis,* especially Ch. II.

24. Quoted in *The Complete Poetical Works of Tennyson,* ed. W. J. Rolfe, p. 198.

25. Allen Ginsberg, *"Howl" and Other Poems,* Pocket Poets Series No. 4 (San Francisco, 1959), p. 9.

26. Henry James, "Tennyson's Drama," *Views and Reviews* (Boston, 1908), p. 165. Tennyson began work on *Queen Mary* in 1874; it was published the following May and had a brief run at the Lyceum Theatre in April and May, 1876.

27. Henry James, "Tennyson's Drama," *Views and Reviews,* p. 165.

28. Ibsen began writing *Pillars of Society* in 1875, the year Tennyson's *Queen Mary* was published. *Ghosts* received its first production in 1882 in the United States, the same year Tennyson's last play, *The Promise of May,* appeared at the Globe Theatre.

29. *The Devil and the Lady,* ed. Sir Charles Tennyson (London, 1930); reprinted along with *Unpublished Early Poems* by Indiana University Press (Bloomington, 1964).

30. *Memoir,* II, 173.

31. *Memoir,* II, 186.

Chapter Five

1. Donald Davie, "Remembering the Thirties," *New and Selected Poems* (Middletown, Conn., 1961), p. 15.

2. W. H. Auden, "Introduction," *A Selection from the Poems of Alfred, Lord Tennyson;* Paull F. Baum, *Tennyson Sixty Years After;* F. L. Lucas, "Tennyson" in *Ten Victorian Poets* (Cambridge, 1948), and *Tennyson,* Writers and Their Work Series (London, 1957); Sir Harold Nicolson, *Tennyson: Aspects of His Life, Character, and Poetry.*

3. Jerome Hamilton Buckley, *Tennyson: The Growth of a Poet,* p. 254.

4. *"In Memoriam," Essays Ancient and Modern,* p. 186.

5. Paull F. Baum, *Tennyson Sixty Years After,* p. 287.

6. Buckley, *Tennyson,* p. 169.

7. *The Works of John Ruskin,* ed. Cook and Wedderburn (London, 1904), V, 362, n. 1.

8. Valerie Pitt, *Tennyson Laureate,* p. 269.

9. Sir Harold Nicolson, *Tennyson,* Anchor edition, p. 324.

10. *The Correspondence of Gerard Manley Hopkins and Richard Watson Dixon,* ed. Claude Colleer Abbott (London, 1935), p. 25.
11. Milton Millhauser, "Structure and Symbol in 'Crossing the Bar,'" *Victorian Poetry,* IV (1966), 35.
12. Buckley, *Tennyson,* pp. 243–44.
13. Millhauser, p. 36.
14. Elton Edward Smith, *The Two Voices: A Tennyson Study,* p. 200.
15. James R. Kincaid, "Tennyson's 'Crossing the Bar'; A Poem of Frustration," *Victorian Poetry,* III (1965), 61.
16. Laurence Perrine, "When Does Hope Mean Doubt?: The Tone of 'Crossing the Bar,'" *Victorian Poetry,* IV (1966), 130–131.

Selected Bibliography

A brief bibliography of Tennyson must exclude many more important items than it can list; some additional references of general interest may be gleaned from my footnotes. Among the bibliographies noted below are both selective and exhaustive compilations. I have deliberately slighted here the earlier Tennyson criticism, which is voluminous.

The musical and curious may be interested in a couple of settings of Tennyson's poems: Benjamin Britten's *Serenade for Tenor, Horn, and Strings,* Opus 31, includes the "Bugle Song" from *The Princess.* Richard Strauss's *"Enoch Arden," Melodrama for Voice and Pianoforte,* Opus 38, is a declamation with musical accompaniment. Both works have been recorded.

PRIMARY SOURCES

Editions

The Collected Editions of Tennyson's works are numerous. The Cambridge Poets Edition (Boston: Houghton Mifflin, 1898, ed. by W. J. Rolfe) which I have used whenever possible is handy because of its inclusion of Alfred's probable contributions to *Poems by Two Brothers* and of discarded and uncollected poems, as well as many passages from poems later revised; but it is not complete. *The Works of Tennyson Annotated* (London and New York: Macmillan, 1907–1908, ed. by Hallam, Lord Tennyson), the "Eversley Edition" in nine volumes, contains notes by Tennyson and his son. Sir Charles Tennyson's editions of *The Devil and the Lady* and *Unpublished Early Poems* have been reissued in a single volume (Bloomington: Indiana University Press, 1964). An edition of the poems (exclusive of the plays) undertaken by Christopher Ricks for the Longmans Annotated English Poets series should prove extremely valuable.

Of the many volumes of selections, three may be mentioned. *A Selection from the Poems of Alfred, Lord Tennyson,* ed. by W. H. Auden (Garden City, N. Y.: Doubleday, 1944) is a slap-dash wartime edition, but the selection is interesting, and Auden's bold and provocative introduction is justly noted. *Poems by Tennyson,* ed. by Jerome H. Buckley (Boston: Houghton Mifflin Riverside Editions, 1958) is a splendid selection with a useful introduction. *Alfred Lord Tennyson: Selected Poetry,* ed. by Herbert Marshall McLuhan (New York: Holt, Rinehart, and Winston Rinehart Editions, 1956) contains some factual errors, but McLuhan's view of Tennyson is a stimulating one.

SECONDARY SOURCES

BAKER, ARTHUR E. *A Concordance to the Poetical and Dramatic Works of Alfred, Lord Tennyson.* New York: Barnes and Noble, 1966. A reprint of the 1914 Macmillan edition.

BAUM, PAULL F. *Tennyson Sixty Years After.* Chapel Hill: University of North Carolina Press, 1948. Though Baum's *ennuyé* manner can annoy, it never obscures the trenchancy of his judgments. This remains one of the solidest general studies of Tennyson's work.

BRADLEY, A. C. *A Commentary on Tennyson's* In Memoriam. London: Macmillan, 1901. Best of several rather old-fashioned book-length guides to the poem's structure and meaning.

BUCKLEY, JEROME HAMILTON. *Tennyson: The Growth of a Poet.* Cambridge: Harvard University Press, 1960. Authoritative and appreciative. It does not, however, justify the view of Tennyson's career implied by the subtitle.

———. *Victorian Poets and Prose Writers.* Goldentree Bibliographies. New York: Appleton-Century-Crofts, 1966. Includes a quite up-to-date though limited Tennyson bibliography.

BUSH, DOUGLAS. *Mythology and the Romantic Tradition.* Cambridge: Harvard University Press, 1937. The Tennyson chapter not only discusses his poems on mythological subjects but is, in its own right, a splendid general essay on Tennyson as a poet who mastered his craft and its tradition.

CADBURY, WILLIAM. "Tennyson's 'The Palace of Art' and the Rhetoric of Structures." *Criticism,* VII (1965), 23–44. In arguing that "the poem is about change, not about art," Cadbury examines it as "an imitation of a pattern of feeling" similar to that of *In Memoriam, Maud,* and *Idylls of the King.*

CARR, ARTHUR J. "Tennyson as a Modern Poet." *University of Toronto Quarterly,* XIX (1950), 361–82. Masterful exploration of Tennyson's sensibility and the poetical "strategies" it employed. Posits a poet of feeling and conscience, rather than of system and principle, who "triumphs not as a master but as a victim."

ELIOT, T. S. "*In Memoriam.*" *Essays Ancient and Modern.* New York: Harcourt Brace, 1936. A perceptive account of the poem's religious mood and its technical merit. "Tennyson is the great master of metric as well as of melancholia."

HOUGH, GRAHAM. "The Natural Theology of *In Memoriam*." *Review of English Studies*, XXIII (1947), 244–56. Traces the religious argument of *In Memoriam* to its sources in the writings of such scientists as Lyell, the influence of Coleridge, and Tennyson's own "mystical" intuitions.

JAPISKE, CORNELIA G. *The Dramas of Alfred, Lord Tennyson*. London: Macmillan, 1926. There is no really adequate treatment of Tennyson as a dramatist.

JOHNSON, E. D. H. "Alfred, Lord Tennyson," in *Victorian Poets: A Guide to Research*, ed. by Frederic E. Faverty. 2nd edition, Cambridge: Harvard University Press, 1968. Bibliographical essay on Tennyson scholarship and criticism.

———. *The Alien Vision of Victorian Poetry*. Princeton, N. J.: Princeton University Press, 1952. Considers Tennyson, along with the other major Victorians, as a poet struggling between the two worlds of public *mores* and personal insight.

JUMP, J. D., ed. *Tennyson: The Critical Heritage*. London: Routledge and Kegan Paul, 1967. Collection of nineteenth-century critical notices of Tennyson's poetry.

KILLHAM, JOHN, ed. *Critical Essays on the Poetry of Tennyson*. London: Routledge and Kegan Paul; N. Y.: Barnes and Noble, 1960. A handy collection (with an excellent introduction) of some of the most valuable modern criticism, including many of the items listed in this bibliography.

KILLHAM, JOHN. *Tennyson and "The Princess": Reflections of an Age*. London: Athlone Press, University of London, 1958. Reviews the concerns of the time regarding the role of women and other matters to which the poem was a serious response.

KISSANE, JAMES. "Tennyson: The Passion of the Past and the Curse of Time." *ELH, A Journal of English Literary History*, XXXII (1965), 85–109. Discusses Tennyson's longing to recover the past for a barren present as a shaping power in much of his important poetry.

LANGBAUM, ROBERT. *The Poetry of Experience*. New York: Random House, 1957. Original and illuminating consideration of the dramatic monologue, including Tennyson's work in that form.

LUCAS, F. L. *Tennyson*. London: Longmans Green, 1957. This short, crisp critical biography offers a very shrewd summing up.

MARSHALL, GEORGE O., JR. *A Tennyson Handbook*. New York: Twayne, 1964. A most useful source of factual material on each of Tennyson's poems. Includes a bibliography.

MATTES, ELEANOR B. *In Memoriam, the Way of a Soul: A Study of Some Influences that Shaped Tennyson's Poem*. New York: Exposition Press, 1951. Valuable material on the intellectual background and structure of the poem and on the probable date of composition of individual sections.

MAYS, J. C. C. "*In Memoriam:* An Aspect of Form." *University of Toronto Quarterly,* XXXV (1965), 22–46. Tennyson's attitude toward "form," especially in relation to "faith," is expressed in the structure of the poem. A brilliant yet commonsensical essay.

NICOLSON, SIR HAROLD. *Tennyson: Aspects of His Life, Character, and Poetry.* London: Constable, 1923. Also, Anchor Books, Garden City: Doubleday, 1962 (includes an "Afterword"). Though Nicolson's characterization of Tennyson as "unhappy mystic" (admirable) and "prosperous Victorian" (deplorable) seems both dated and oversimplified, this study is still rewarding for its many acute perceptions and its sparkling literacy.

PADEN, W. D. *Tennyson in Egypt: A Study of the Imagery in His Earlier Work.* Lawrence, Kan.: University of Kansas Press, 1942. Adds to the method of Lowes's *The Road to Xanadu* some psychoanalytic embellishments.

PITT, VALERIE. *Tennyson Laureate.* London: Barrie and Rockliff, 1962. Attempts to place Tennyson's "sense of the common and the social" on equal footing with his private sensitivities in an assessment of his work.

PRIESTLEY, F. E. L. "Tennyson's *Idylls.*" *University of Toronto Quarterly,* XIX (1949), 35–49. Explication of the moral themes that give coherence to the *Idylls.* (See Ch. III, n. 26.)

PYRE, J. F. A. *The Formation of Tennyson's Style: A Study, Primarily, of the Versification of the Early Poems.* Madison: University of Wisconsin Press, 1921. Rather pedestrian.

RADER, RALPH W. *Tennyson's* Maud: *The Biographical Genesis.* Berkeley: University of California Press, 1963. Sheds important light on young Tennyson's attractions to Rosa Baring, Sophy Rawnsley, and Emily Sellwood and traces the effect of these upon his poetry —especially *Maud.*

RAWNSLEY, H. D. *Memories of the Tennysons.* Glasgow: Maclehose, 1900. Reminiscences by a close family acquaintance.

RICHARDSON, JOANNA. *The Pre-Eminent Victorian: A Study of Tennyson.* London: Cape, 1962. A sympathetic biography concentrating on the laureate period (after 1850).

ROSENBERG, JOHN D. "The Two Kingdoms of *In Memoriam.*" *Journal of English and Germanic Philology,* LVIII (1959), 228–40. Combines shrewd analysis with sound evaluation, though perhaps the "two kingdoms" of evolutionary science and Christian faith are less intermixed in the poem than Rosenberg suggests.

RYALS, CLYDE DE L. *From the Great Deep: Essays on the* Idylls of the

King. Athens: Ohio University Press, 1967. Treats various aspects of form and meaning by way of arguing for the poem's complexity and Tennyson's sophistication as a thinker.

———. *Theme and Symbol in Tennyson's Poems to 1850.* Philadelphia: University of Pennsylvania Press, 1964. Stresses Tennyson's "divided personality" in tracing recurrent themes and symbols through the early poetry, culminating in *In Memoriam.*

SHANNON, EDGAR F., JR. *Tennyson and the Reviewers: A Study of His Literary Reputation and of the Influence of the Critics upon His Poetry, 1821–1851.* Cambridge: Harvard University Press, 1952. Contains much important information, including a list of early reviews of Tennyson's poetry.

SMITH, ELTON EDWARD. *The Two Voices: A Tennyson Study.* Lincoln: University of Nebraska Press, 1964. Discusses the poetry in terms of seven—mainly thematic—antitheses. Often bogs down in the recital of other critics' opinions.

STEVENSON, LIONEL. *Darwin Among the Poets.* Chicago: University of Chicago Press, 1932. Chapter on Tennyson is a thorough treatment of Tennyson's relation to natural science and philosophy.

TENNYSON, SIR CHARLES. *Alfred Tennyson.* New York: Macmillan, 1949. The standard biography. Illuminates the circumstances of Alfred's childhood, especially his father's instability.

———. *Six Tennyson Essays.* London: Cassell, 1954. Poet's grandson knowledgeably expounds a variety of subjects, including Tennyson's humor, politics, religion, and versification.

TENNYSON, SIR CHARLES AND FALL, CHRISTINE. *Alfred Tennyson: An Annotated Bibliography.* Athens: University of Georgia Press, 1967. Thorough listing of Tennyson studies through 1964.

TENNYSON, HALLAM, LORD. *Alfred, Lord Tennyson: A Memoir,* 2 vols. New York: Macmillan, 1897. Primary source of information, compiled by the poet's son.

WILLEY, BASIL. "Tennyson," *More Nineteenth Century Studies.* London: Chatto and Windus, 1956. Excellent brief summary of Tennyson's career through *In Memoriam.* Places him among the century's "honest doubters."

YOUNG, G. M. "The Age of Tennyson." *Victorian Essays.* London: Oxford University Press, 1962. Humane and acute appreciation by one of the greatest students of Victorian culture.

Index

65, 132-135